THE CEO'S COMPASS

How to Navigate Your Team Through Turbulent Times

Jonathan Bowman-Perks MBE

TM

The CEO's Compass: How to Navigate Your Team Through Turbulent Times

First edition printed and published in the United Kingdom 2025.

A CIP catalogue record of this book is available from the British Library.

ISBN: 978-1-9191712-0-3 (Hardcover)
ISBN: 978-1-9191712-1-0 (Paperback)
Imprint: Inspiring Leadership International Limited
Editors: Christine Beech, Harriet Soni and David Sloly
Typesetting: Matthew J Bird

The CEO's Compass™ and The CEO's Compass image™:
Trademarks: Inspiring Leadership International Limited

For further information about this book, please contact the author - jp@jonathanperks.com
Visit his website for more information www.jonathanperks.com

Dedication

For my family:
My wife, my anchor through every storm, Leigh
My children, Harriet and Bryony
My stepchildren, Daniel and Alanadh
Their husbands and wives, Sandeep, Mark, Kirsty and Liam
My grandchildren, Lyra and Sofia
My step-grandchildren, Grace and Riley
My brothers, David (in memory) and Graeme (my mentor)

Each of you reminds me daily what truly matters
You are my True North
You are my legacy
I love you

In memory of:
My parents, Tricia and Paul

To them I owe all that I am, and the values I hold

Contents

THE CEO'S COMPASS

How to Navigate Your Team Through Turbulent Times

Preface
The Burning Why:
Setting the CEO's Compass

"Jonathan, you have ten years left to live."

The cardiologist did not mince words. The news landed like a hammer blow, unvarnished and impossible to ignore. For sixty-two years, I had been living with a hidden congenital heart defect, undetected by every military medical check-up, every challenge and every test.

The right chambers of my heart are enlarged and failing. There's no miracle fix. Just the clock, ticking.

Moments like this test everything you think you know. The mission shifts. The stakes become real. Suddenly, you're faced with a choice:

Define yourself, or let the moment define you.

In his book, *'Man's Search for Meaning,'* **Viktor Frankl** quotes **Nietzsche**:

> **"He who has a why to live for can bear almost any how."**

That day, I made three resolutions:

Family:
I will keep loving them wholeheartedly, and ensure I'm always there for them when they need me.

Purpose:
I will lead with everything I have, coaching, serving and shaping leaders, for as long as I am able to.

Legacy:
I will pass on leadership lessons I've learned in the hardest moments.

Wisdom only matters if it's shared. I determined to write this book and donate the profits to my wife's charity, *The Inspiring Leadership Foundation*, serving the most disadvantaged.

Fear will not write my final chapter. I will lead with courage, as I have always hoped to, just as my father did before me.

On the Shoulders of Giants: The Power of Shared Wisdom

Let me share a simple truth with you: no leader, no matter how seasoned, walks this path alone. Writing this book was never a solitary pursuit.

Over the years, I've had the privilege of sitting down with more than 400 remarkable, inspiring leaders on my *Inspiring Leadership Podcast*. Each conversation offered a window into the heart of leadership. Together, we stripped away the veneer and revealed raw stories - the triumphs, the failures and the hard-won lessons.

Chapter 10 includes a full list of the first 400 podcasts and details on how to access each episode. As you read, you'll find stories, moments of insight and references from my distinguished guests.

Each story is a beacon to guide you on your own journey. Research gives you facts, but stories give you wisdom. In the boardroom, as on the battlefield, it is wisdom that truly lights the way.

I share these voices because their wisdom shaped mine, and I believe it will shape yours too. It is with their expressed permission that I share their experiences and setbacks, which they turned into stepping stones for success.

Your Growth Mindset

As you read, know this: you are not alone. You are surrounded by leaders who have faced the same storms, wrestled the same doubts, and emerged stronger. Their stories are now yours to draw from, just as I have.

They will give you the courage and confidence to accept the following challenge:

"Attack life, don't let it attack you."

This attitude is drawn from someone who has faced raw adversity, stared down the worst pit of depression and emerged with an unbreakable spirit: **Toby Gutteridge** (*Podcast 393*). Toby is a remarkably inspiring leader. An elite Tier 1 Special Boat Service (SBS) soldier turned business visionary, his life changed in an instant when he was shot through the neck in Afghanistan, leaving him quadriplegic.

As the author of *Never Will I Die,* Toby has not only endured life's toughest challenges, but he has also defied them. He told me:

"If I empowered and intrigued [others] with my stories, they returned the favour by reminding me what it was like to attack life, as opposed to being overwhelmed by it."

There's a quiet power in those words. Toby's perspective is not just about surviving. It's about *choosing* - choosing to meet each day head-on, with intention, with courage. It was with this courage, he shared:

"I had come to terms with my limitations and stopped being defined by them."

In business, as in life, it's all too easy to let the relentless tide of demands and crises sweep you along. Yet real leaders, those who truly inspire teams, shape cultures, and leave lasting legacies, are the ones who refuse to be overwhelmed.

They attack life. They set the agenda. They define the vision. They move with purpose, even when the odds are stacked against them.

The true measure of your leadership is not found in the easy days. It's revealed in how fiercely you choose to live, and to lead, when the stakes are highest.

The Compass Model

Whether in the heat of military operations, or the pressure cooker of corporate life, our instinctive response to crises is *fight, flight, freeze, or fawn*. When the stakes are high, the mind narrows, options shrink, and leadership is put to the test.

Yet, there is no magic silver bullet to leadership. No universal truth that says, *"Do this in all situations"*. Leadership is contextual. It depends on your people, your organisation, your sector - your moment. What works for one leader, in one company, in one climate, may fail for another.

That's why you need more than tactics. You need a bedrock of principles, values, and a framework for thinking clearly when the pressure is on.

After decades leading teams in uniform and coaching executives in business, I saw the need for this repeat itself, time and again. It's why Leigh and I created *The CEO's Compass:* a framework for finding your True North, so you can inspire others to follow - even when the way ahead is murky, uncertain, or changing by the hour. It's why I chose The CEO's Compass for this book.

It's practical, it's proven, and it's built on over 40 years of leadership lessons, in-depth interviews and real-world experience, blending military precision with business acumen. It's your leadership Swiss Army knife, a trusted companion for navigating uncertainty, making tough calls and inspiring your team to greatness.

Danny Payne CMG, former CEO of the Foreign and Commonwealth Office Services (*Podcast 54*), knows what it means to lead through turbulence. He described this book as:

"A guide through tough times and a reminder of what really matters and what does not. When all around are stressed and losing perspective, it becomes my grounding force. I draw on my previous mistakes, wisdom and experience to provide clarity when there is so much uncertainty."

Admiral Sir Nick Hine KCB, CEO Babcock Marine and former 2nd Sea Lord (*Podcast 351*) called it:

> *"A leader's battle-hardened compass and mentor in your pocket."*

Leadership isn't about never feeling lost. It's about having the right compass when you are.

Charting Your Own Course

I remember it vividly: A rain-soaked wood. Boots heavy with mud. Breath sharp in the cold air as I waited for an RAF Chinook to lift me to my next operation.

Beside me stood my commanding officer - now **General The Lord Dannatt GCB CBE MC DL** (*Podcast 200*). He turned and asked me a deceptively simple question:

> *"What's your plan for your life?"*

I admitted, truthfully, I didn't have one.

He didn't miss a beat. He looked me in the eye and said,

> *"If you don't chart your own course, you'll end up following someone else's. And, trust me, their plan for you isn't much."*

That lesson hit hard. In business, as in life, if you don't set your own direction, someone else will. Leadership demands that you take the wheel, define your path and build a legacy on your terms.

You don't control the storms. You control your response. So, you set your compass. You trust your training. Then you take the next step, no matter how rough the seas become.

My hope is that these pages help you chart your own course, guide your team through adversity and build an enduring legacy, one worthy of your journey.

Let's get to work.

1
MQ – Moral Quotient:
Find Your True North

What is MQ?

Leadership starts with a True North: your values and principles. You live and lead by a clear set of beliefs that guide every decision and every action. Whether you're commanding a platoon or steering a boardroom, your integrity remains one of your greatest assets. People watch what you do far more than what you say.

When your actions are consistent, your word becomes your bond. Trust follows naturally.

A Personal Story - Compassion Over Comfort

My earliest lesson in moral intelligence didn't come from a textbook. It came in the back of my mother's old car, after church one Sunday.

My brothers and I were squeezed in the back, after my mother pulled over for an old homeless lady. The lady's hair was matted, her breath sour, her teeth brown, her coat threadbare. She smelled of urine. It would have been easy to look away; to pretend we hadn't seen her. But my mother didn't hesitate. She invited the woman to lunch with us. We shared a meal and, for that moment, she was no longer invisible.

That day taught me to see the person, not the problem. To act with compassion, not judgment. True leadership is grounded in respect, regardless of status or circumstance. It isn't about comfort or convenience. It's about doing the right thing, even when it's awkward, or costly. It's about making the hard choices, holding the line, and setting the standard for others to follow.

Standards Demand Discipline

When I think of integrity and values-led excellence in business, I think of **Horst Schulze**, founder of the Ritz-Carlton Hotel chain (*Podcast 294*). He built his legacy on a simple, uncompromising standard:

> *"Excellence is not an accident. It's the result of high intent, hard work and living in accordance with your values. Your destiny is shaped by the decisions you make in life."*

In business, as in the military, your standards define you.

Admiral Bill McRaven (*Podcast 340*) possesses the same commitment to setting a high bar. He masterminded the raid that brought down Osama bin Laden, commanded the capture of Saddam Hussein and led countless high-stake missions as Head of the U.S. Special Operations Command. He has turned adversity into strength and led with clarity.

I urge you to read his books, especially *Conquering Crisis*. He's been a great, inspiring role model to me and many leaders. In our podcast, Bill distilled a lifetime's wisdom in uniform into one powerful truth:

> *"If you want to change the world, you must be your very best in the darkest moments."*

As a leader, your legacy is built through resolve and clarity. Set your bearings. Hold your course. The journey to inspiring leadership begins with your unwavering True North.

Beware of Drift

Every leader faces a choice between True North - your core values and authentic purpose - and Magnetic North - the shifting distractions, pressures, and external influences that can pull you off course. The difference may seem tiny - just a fraction of a degree - but over time, that small deviation can take you miles off course.

I've seen it in the military and the boardroom. Leaders whose values drift as outside pressure builds - one shortcut here, a quiet compromise there. It doesn't look like much at first, but one day, they find themselves far from the beliefs and integrity they once lived by. The damage isn't instant. But over time, it corrodes judgment, erodes reputation and affects the culture you're meant to protect.

Anil Kanti (Neil) Basu, former Assistant Commissioner for Specialist Operations and UK Counter Terrorism (*Podcasts 326 and 390*), saw this firsthand. In his book, *Turmoil*, he describes surviving a *'FIFO: Fit In or F*** Off'* culture as a man of colour in the Metropolitan Police. Early on, he tried to blend in, ignoring toxic behaviour just to get through. But as he rose through the ranks, he found his voice - and his True North. He led the Stephen Lawrence inquiry and responded to the George Floyd Murder. Each time, he stood for integrity and values, even when it meant standing alone. Anil Kanti told me:

> *"Without your True North, you disintegrate."*

He's right. If you aren't clear about what you stand for, you'll fall for anything. Others sense this uncertainty and trust can vanish quickly. Values aren't just personal - they're contagious. A leader's consistent integrity, or lack of it, sets the tone for the entire organisation. Harvard Professor **Bill George** put it simply in his book *True North:*

> *"Find your True North and never stray from it."*

That's the challenge for every leader.

Set Your Guardrails

To maintain consistency, every business leader needs guardrails - firm boundaries that you will not cross, no matter the pressure. In leadership, the hardest decisions often exist in the grey areas, not in black and white. The personal standards you uphold, especially when uncertainty strikes or the stakes are high, are what shape your legacy.

Guy Hands, Founder of Terra Firma (*Podcast 187*), learned this through triumph and setback in the unforgiving world of Private Equity:

> *"You need to walk the talk, not just talk the talk. And you have to be willing to not compromise on certain red lines. Otherwise, why would anyone follow you?"*

Guardrails - your non-negotiable lines - become an operational advantage. They give your team confidence you'll stand firm when it matters most.

Rhetoric Versus Reality

We've all heard the speeches about ethics and values, but words are easy. **Roger Steare** (*Podcast 25*), author of *Ethicability: How to Decide What's Right and Find the Courage to Do It*, has researched the gap between what organisations say and what they actually do. Trust is lost in that gap - the space between rhetoric and reality. Our task, as leaders, is to close it.

People don't judge you by your promises. They judge you by your actions. Your reputation is not just built in one grand, heroic moment. It's built over the thousands of small choices and the standards you uphold when no one's watching.

Mike Still (*Podcast 33*), Managing Director and crisis-tested leader, is clear:

> *"Integrity is not just about honesty - it's about living your values consistently, especially when no one is watching."*

Integrity is proven under pressure. The best leaders live it every day - it's not measured by what is easy, but by what is hard.

Questions for You

Take a hard look at your leadership:

- Are your values visible in your daily actions?
- Does your team know what you stand for - without you having to say it?

Marcus Aurelius in his *Meditations* posed a simple challenge:

> *"When you've done well and another has benefited by it, why like a fool do you look for a third thing on top - credit for the good deed or a favour in return?"*

Do the right thing because it is right, not for credit.

When Your Values Slip

There have been times I've let my standards slip and disappointed those who trusted me. I've learned that integrity isn't about *being perfect*. It's about being honest, owning your mistakes and setting a higher standard next time. Today, my core values are non-negotiable. I'd rather answer any question and know I have nothing to hide.

Larry English, CEO of Centric Consulting (*Podcast 153*), shares this philosophy:

> *"For me, it's all about honesty, integrity and hard work. These are the values I live by and they are non-negotiable. Sure, I've stumbled and strayed from them at times - we all do. But my beliefs always bring me back on track. Stick to your values and you'll find your way."*

When your integrity is questioned, you can't hide from it. You must act. If people doubt your word, set it right, and do it fast.

Colonel Andy Milburn, U.S. Marines Special Forces and author of '*When the Tempest Gathers*' (*Podcast 287*) is blunt:

> *"It is important to call out bad behaviour, rather than be a bystander condoning it. Always have that moral courage and integrity to admit if you've done something wrong. So, you stick your hand up and say, 'Yeah, you know what? I'm very sorry. I've done it. I've messed up. Let me try and make this right'."*

That is the standard. In business, as in the military, it is not enough to avoid doing wrong. You need to own your mistakes, call out the unacceptable and set the tone for your team. Leadership is not about *never* making mistakes - it's about what you do next. When you slip, admit it. Apologise. Learn from it. Set a new standard. That's how you close the gap between rhetoric and reality. That's how you build trust that endures.

Openness and Trust

My great friend, **Jeff Nischwitz** (*Podcasts 138 and 332*), is a leadership coach, facilitator and a masterful leader of the ManKind Project. He captured another truth in three phrases that every leader should have the courage to say:

- *I was wrong*
- *I don't know*
- *I need some help*

Simple to say, but they demand real strength. In the military, admitting fallibility is not weakness - it is the bedrock of trust. In business, it is the difference between a culture of fear and one of innovation and high performance. Weak leaders hide behind perfection. Strong leaders admit fault, uncertainty, and need, and in doing so, earn lasting trust.

Jason Fox - Royal Marines and Special Forces veteran, now TV presenter for *SAS: Who Dares Wins* (*Podcast 353*) - has faced adversity few can imagine. He told me:

> *"I don't need to lie about putting up a make-believe bravado to feed my ego. My cards are on the table. This is me. I've nothing to hide anymore."*

Authenticity builds psychological safety in teams, freeing people to share their needs and mistakes openly.

Captain David Marquet (*Podcast 120*), turned the USS Santa Fe into the fleet's best-performing submarine by creating an environment where everyone was trusted to act with integrity:

"If you want people to think, give them intent, not instructions. When you do, moral integrity becomes the backbone of every decision."

This comes from putting ego aside. **Lieutenant General James Bashall CB CBE** (*Podcasts 32 and 61*) and I once shared the hardships of Airborne training. He put it best:

"Humility is a really important quality to keep."

True leadership is not about seeking the spotlight. It is about setting the tone through your example.

LEADERSHIP WISDOM

Angie Klein, CEO of Visible (*Podcast 75*), runs the Verizon-owned company with a reputation for no-nonsense drive and unwavering integrity. She said:

"It's not what you accomplish that makes you a leader. It is how you pursue it and how you go about it that actually inspires others. Are you doing it with integrity?"

For Angie, real leaders inspire through the way they chase their goals - bringing people along, never stepping over them. Integrity becomes the guardrail that earns trust and loyalty. The path you choose matters as much as the destination. Walk it with integrity and people will follow, not because they have to, but because they want to.

YOUR CALL TO ACTION

Stand in front of the mirror and ask yourself, out loud:

"What do I do when I let my values slip?"

- Pause and reflect
- Write down three lessons you have learned from those slips
- Share them with someone you trust

The best leaders are not flawless. They own their mistakes, learn quickly and set a new standard. Vulnerability is not weakness; it's the cornerstone of trust.

To strengthen your credibility and build trust, practice those three phrases:

- *I was wrong*
- *I don't know*
- *I need some help*

Your team will see real strength, real openness. Openness replaces fear, learning replaces blame. Try this at your next team off-site. Challenge everyone to use those ten words. You'll get real conversations, real trust, real progress.

This is the mark of a world-class leader: making it safe to speak the truth, ask for help and grow stronger together, no matter how rough things get.

YOUR NEXT MISSION

Each element of your *CEO's Compass* is connected. **Moral Intelligence (MQ)** is the anchor - steady when pressure mounts or the future is unclear. Without it, strategy falters. The next chapter is **Purpose Quotient (PQ)**, the force behind every decision you make.

Stephen M. R. Covey (*Podcast 299*), bestselling author of *The Speed of Trust* shaped corporate and government thinking when he said:

"Live your life by a compass, not a clock."

To Stephen, leadership means being steered by your values, not just your deadlines. When you align with your True North, you build trust and drive culture. Let your compass, not your clock, set your course.

Ralph Waldo Emerson summed it up:

> *"Sow a thought and you reap an act. Sow an act and you reap a habit. Sow a habit and you reap a character. Sow a character and you reap a destiny."*

Your purpose and integrity are crafted one decision at a time.
Make each one count.

2
PQ – Purpose Quotient:
Ignite Passion and Define Your Vocation

What is PQ?

Purpose is the driving force behind great leadership. It's your "why". It's not just about hitting targets or chasing success. It's about making your work matter. Purpose gives you clarity. It's knowing what you stand for, why you fight for it and why you show up every day. I often share Mark Twain's wisdom with CEOs and executive teams:

"The two most important days in your life are the day you are born and the day you discover your 'why'."

When you find your "why", everything sharpens. Your mission becomes clear, your values and vision snap into focus and your team feels it, because purpose is contagious. In coaching leaders, the same themes surface again and again:

Create a clear vision, build meaning at work, help people find personal purpose.

Sophie Neary, Managing Director at Google and a trailblazing executive with over 30 years of leadership experience at Meta, Boots, Tesco, and Asda (*Podcast 177*), put it profoundly:

"When we know our purpose in the world, that's when we begin to live a meaningful life. That's when we find true fulfilment - not just temporary pleasure."

Seamus Smith, Group President at FIS (*Podcast 161*), a powerhouse of energy and focus, told me:

> *"I've been very fortunate in that, for I would say 95% of my professional career, I've done things that I've believed in and aligned with my values and beliefs."*

That alignment is where the magic happens.

Purpose is Built, Not Found

It requires focused, deliberate practice to align your actions, values and beliefs. **Professor Philippa Snare**, Chief Marketing Officer at Microsoft, Meta and now SVP at The Trade Desk (*Podcasts 4 and 101*), shares the importance of this:

> *"To be an inspiring leader, live a life 'on purpose'. Make conscious choices, rather than just going with the flow."*

Leaders who are proactive and intentional set an example which motivates teams towards meaningful goals and inspires them to stay the course.

Sherilyn Shackell, Founder and CEO of The Marketing Academy (*Podcast 44*), has made it her life's work to unlock leadership potential and help others find meaning in their careers. She told me:

> *"Purpose isn't something you find - it's something you build day by day. When your work becomes your calling, every Monday feels like a gift."*

Earlier in my career, I often struggled with confidence in whether I would discover my calling. There were times I felt uncertain about who I really was. Part of me always feared being exposed, as if someone might ask:

> *"Will the real Jonathan please stand up?"*

Here's what I learned: Being comfortable with who you are, truly knowing yourself, is the foundation of living your life on purpose.

Authenticity in Leadership

Peter Kavanagh, Chairman of Leaders Romans Group (*Podcast 47*), built one of the UK's largest privately owned property service companies through honesty, hard work and authenticity. He credits his values to his mother, who taught him to be true to himself and treat people well.
He advised:

> *"Trust and empower the people you work with to make the right decisions. Be brave and, above all, be yourself."*

Peter made it clear: calm, consistent, authentic leadership is what people crave. No one thrives in uncertainty, or under leaders who put ego before the team.

For him, leadership is a privilege, not a platform for self-promotion. Success comes from empowering others and staying grounded in who you are.

Michael Cook, who succeeded Peter as CEO, rose through the ranks from Sales Negotiator to the top role - shaping the business through mergers and sustained growth. His style is rooted in staying true to the organisation's values, fostering trust through transparency and consistency. Working with Peter and Michael showed me this truth: authentic leadership is not about perfection. It is about being genuine, approachable and steadfast in your values. When you lead as your *real self*, you build the foundation needed to pursue a clear leadership purpose. You also earn loyalty and keep it.

The Fuel of Sustainable Success

Srini Gopalan, CEO at T-Mobile USA and former Board Member for Germany at Deutsche Telekom, has transformed businesses and customer experiences in some of the most competitive markets worldwide.
His advice is simple:

> *"Never underestimate the strength that a sense of purpose ignites in an organisation. It's the ingredient for sustainable success."*

For Srini, great leadership is never a solo act. It's about truly understanding your business, focusing on what adds value for customers, and connecting with your people to solve real problems. Not just presenting the slides - listening, then acting.

He believes that passion for your work, a clear sense of purpose, and the humility to learn from everyone around you can turn ordinary teams into champions. Lead with meaning and you don't just create customers, you create *fans*, one experience at a time.

A Personal Story - Trust Begins With Openness

In my work, I have learned a truth I carry into every engagement: leadership is a two-way street. Every meeting, every conversation, is a chance to remove the mask, drop the armour and build real, mutual legitimacy across the table.

Trust is the currency of leadership.
If you want to be trusted, you must first trust others.
If you want respect, you must give it.
If you want openness and vulnerability, you must go there yourself, first.

I will never forget one cold sunny day under a cloudless sky, when a CEO told me they had just learned they had a terminal disease. The news was devastating. In that moment, leadership was not about strategy or performance metrics. It was about presence. It was about empathy. It was about listening, without judgment. That kind of openness is often only possible when trust has already been built.

That conversation happened during one of our walking meetings, a space I've found allows leaders to feel safe enough to voice their deepest fears and concerns. Sometimes, the most powerful thing you can do is simply listen, with a clear mind and an open heart. You don't know exactly how it feels for them. You can't know their private battle, but if you truly listen, you help them carry the load.

And when life shifts, priorities shift. Suddenly, what matters most snaps into sharp focus. Purpose, in that moment, isn't just a concept - it's a lifeline. That was a long, powerful coaching session - one I will always remember. By the end of it, we were both much clearer on what gave our lives true meaning and purpose. By not wearing any "mask", we had forged a deeper bond and a trust that cannot be faked.

Wisdom at the End

The importance of the Purpose Quotient (PQ) comes into sharp focus when you listen to the voices of those at the very end of their journey. **Bronnie Ware**, an Australian palliative care nurse, captured that wisdom in her book, *The Top Five Regrets of the Dying*.

Here are those regrets - a wake-up call for every leader:

- *"I wish I had shown the courage to live a life true to myself, not the life others expected of me."*
  Real leadership means charting your own course.

- *"I wish I hadn't worked so hard."*
  It's easy to lose yourself in the grind - sacrificing time with loved ones for career milestones that may not matter in the end.

- *"I wish I had found the courage to express my feelings."*
  Leadership demands honesty, with yourself and with others. Don't leave truth unsaid until it's too late.

- *"I wish I had stayed in touch with my friends."*
  The higher you climb, the easier it is to drift from those who ground you. Keep those relationships alive.

- *"I wish I had let myself be happier."*
  Too many postpone joy. Let happiness be part of your purpose, not just a distant reward.

The Hon Dan Jarvis MBE MP (*Podcast 217*) has lived this truth. As a leader at the highest levels of national security and public service, rising through the Parachute Regiment, before becoming Minister for Security, his career is marked by courage, sacrifice and his unwavering sense of duty.

He told me:

> *"It was an impossible situation. I was torn between my duty to my country and my responsibility to my wife."*

Dan spoke of the profound turmoil of deploying to Afghanistan while his wife, Caroline, was battling cancer - a test of spirit that few can imagine. The worry, the guilt, the feeling of being unprepared - all while leading others through the uncertainty of conflict. Losing Caroline while still serving was a pain that reshaped him. It gave him a deeper resilience, richer empathy and a fierce commitment to cherish every moment. He emerged from that crucible not diminished, but transformed, more attuned to leading with compassion and finding strength in vulnerability.

His story is a call to every CEO and executive: meaning and purpose aren't found in titles or accolades - they're discovered in how we respond to life's hardest moments.

The Power of Knowing Your 'Why'

As I shared earlier, over twenty years ago my commanding officer asked me a question that changed everything:

> *"What's your plan for your life?"*

The Army gave me a sense of mission, but in business, defining my Purpose Quotient has taken constant reflection. There have been moments I've felt fully on purpose, and others where I drifted.

Today my purpose is clear: To carry forward the legacy my father left me. To learn from great leaders. To share those lessons. Then to serve those with fewer opportunities - through business and philanthropy.

My life purpose is:

Inspiring leadership in CEOs and teams, to enhance the lives of people I may never meet.

Your "why" is your anchor. It is what gives your work meaning. It is what keeps you steady when things get tough.

In many cultures, this is called your "Dharma" - your unique calling, the work only you can do. Find it, and you will find the reason to get up in the morning and the impact you want to make. When your purpose is clear, you build resilience. The daily grind becomes meaningful, not just a routine. Your "why" guides you, motivates you and helps you lead your team through any storm.

Whether you live your life "on purpose" or "off purpose", your sense of meaning is the true measure of your happiness and your success.
As **Dale Carnegie** wisely observed:

> *"Success is getting what you want. Happiness is wanting what you already have."*

Ask yourself:

"What gives my life meaning and purpose? Have I found work that feels like a calling, not just a job? Does it align with my values, my family and my sense of mission?"

The Alternative: Leading With Heart

Too often, I meet highly talented people trapped in roles where they're treated as little more than resources to be used and replaced. That's not leadership. That's not purpose. You might take the cynical view and say that, by design, corporations have no heart. By definition, they could even be considered psychopathic. A corporation is a legal entity - it can own assets, make decisions and generate profits. But it cannot care.

Only people can do that.

If you're not careful, your moral compass can be dulled by a culture that puts shareholders above all else. Ask yourself:

"Is my organisation unconsciously drifting in that direction?"

There is another way. The most rewarding organisations I've worked with - across industries and continents - are led by CEOs who infuse their companies with real heart and soul. These are leaders who care deeply about meaning and purpose and it shows in everything they do. Their vision sets the tone and their values shape the culture. People are drawn to work with them not just because of what they do, but because of who they are.

You can spot a true leader the moment they walk into the room. There is a clarity of purpose, a sense of meaning that radiates from how they speak and, more importantly, how they act. In business and in the military, you instantly know if someone is truly living by their values. It's not just words on a wall - it's visible in every decision, every action, every interaction.

That's exactly what struck me in my early days of working with CEO **Matt Oppenheimer** (*Podcast 43*) and his team at Remitly Global. Since 2011, Matt has led Remitly with a clear mission and unwavering sense of purpose, setting the tone that *"every customer matters and every voice is heard"* - often personally handling customer issues and listening to their stories.

Founded to serve immigrants, Remitly now moves money across borders to empower a global community of people excluded by traditional banks. Their Purpose Quotient isn't about chasing the next dollar, or padding the bottom line. Their vision is a call to action:

"Serve those who need it most - and do it with integrity and heart."

The Growth Challenge

When **Matt Oppenheimer** and **Josh Hug** (*Podcast 210*) launched Remitly, their purpose was crystal clear. But as the company grew, the challenge changed. Growth brings new people, structures and stakeholders, and with scale comes risk - the risk of losing the original spark that made you special.

For every CEO, the biggest threat isn't just competition - it's drifting from your founding mission. The more you grow, the harder it becomes to maintain a deep connection to your purpose, your customers, your culture. When you lose your direction, you risk losing the soul of your company.

Your job as CEO is to keep your team anchored to what matters most. Hire people who share your values and live them daily. Protect your culture fiercely. Growth should amplify your purpose, not dilute it. That's what Matt strives to do, and that's what you must do too - because purpose is not a luxury for good times. It is your True North, your competitive advantage and your cultural anchor.

Hold Fast to Your True North

Every challenge is a test. A test of your alignment with your mission and values. Ask yourself regularly:

"Are we still adding real value for our customers?"
"Are our actions true to our founding principles?"

If you lose sight of your purpose, you can get lost in the noise. Stay true to your values and mission, and you will guide your business through any storm.

Meaning and Purpose in the Age of AI

As AI advances, some call this era *"the twilight of human intellectual supremacy"*. Experts warn that soon, machines may surpass us in almost every cognitive task. This prompts a profound question:

If technology can think for us, what gives our work meaning? What will keep us relevant in a world where billions could be replaced by AI?

The answer is purpose. In an age where technical skills can be replicated by algorithms, your "why" remains uniquely human. Purpose drives creativity, judgment, empathy, and ethical leadership. Machines may process data, but only *you* can bring vision, values and meaning to your work and to your team. To stay relevant, keep learning new skills, but above all, lead with purpose. Meaning makes your leadership irreplaceable.

LEADERSHIP WISDOM

Dame Alison Nimmo, CEO of The Crown Estate (*Podcast 2*), is known for her humility and her remarkable impact. She oversaw £14 billion in assets, delivered record returns to the UK Treasury, and led major regeneration projects. She told me a story that goes straight to the heart of leadership:

"I was inspired by Sir Howard Bernstein, CEO of Manchester City Council, when we were rebuilding Manchester after the IRA bombing in 1996. Until then, I thought you went to work because you got paid to go to work. But Sir Howard taught me the power of purpose - getting up every morning to do something you believed in - and not stopping until the city was rebuilt. That personal motivation and commitment is what I've carried on into The Crown Estate."

In a world changing faster than ever, purpose is your anchor. It keeps you and your team motivated, resilient and ready for whatever comes next.

YOUR CALL TO ACTION

Every leader inherits a map, shaped by parents, mentors and early experiences.

But you do not have to follow someone else's route. Great leaders redraw the map. Think back to when you were eight years old. Whose map were you using then? How did it shape your beliefs, your values, your habits? Now ask yourself:

"Does that old map still serve me?"

One of the most powerful things you can do is to adapt your map. Draw from your own experience and from the lessons of those you respect. Choose your mentors and role models with intention.

As **Seneca** wrote:

"We are in the habit of saying that it was not in our power to choose the parents who were allotted to us, that they were given to us by chance. But we can choose whose children we would like to be."

In business and in life, you must personalise your Life Map.

Practical Life Map Exercise

Here's a practical exercise I use with CEOs and executive teams:

1. **Draw Your Life Map**
   Take a blank sheet of paper. On the x-axis, sketch a line from your birth to your current age. On the y-axis, plot your life events - positive experiences above the line, setbacks below. Mark at least three peaks (successes) and three valleys (setbacks). Next to each, jot down what happened and how it shaped you as a leader.

2. **Reflect and learn**
   Step back. Ask, *"So what?"* What did each peak and valley teach you? How did you respond and what strengths did you develop? If you're brave, talk it through with someone you trust.

3. **Decide what comes next**
   Given what you've learned, what is the next step on your map? What will you do differently as a leader? Set one clear action and commit to it.

Those who master their map earn respect - not just for their achievements, but for their self-awareness and resilience. Leaders who learn from every peak and valley are more grounded, more balanced and better equipped to guide others through uncertainty. You can't control the map you were handed, but you can control the one you draw from here.

Your Life Line:
Exercise

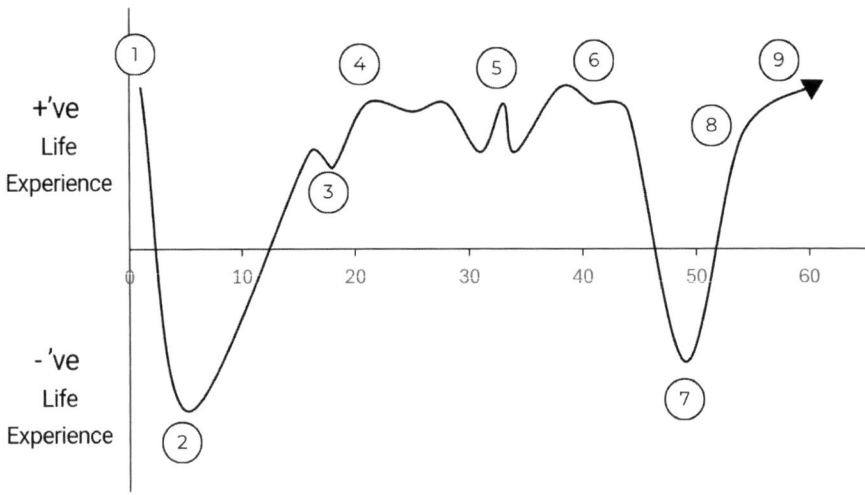

1. Parents blissfully happily married + 3 children
2. Father RN Fast Jet Pilot killed flying
3. Joined British Army
4. Won World Record mountain marathon in Cyprus
5. Graduated Army staff college then MBE
6. Left Army with MBA into business PwC
7. Divorce
8. Now married to Leigh. 4 married children + 4 grandchildren
9. Appreciate my family, my work, the ILF charity + Podcast

Setting Your Why

Ask yourself:

- *"What gives my life meaning and purpose?"*
- *"Why do I do what I do?"*
- *"What percentage of my time am I living on purpose?"*
- *"How will I prepare for the impact of disruptors on my job and industry?"*

Share your answers with someone you trust. Each week, check in: *"Am I living on purpose - or drifting?"* If you drift, then adjust.

Take your team through this exercise. At your next off-site, clarify your shared sense of meaning. This is not a tick-box activity; it's where trust, resilience and alignment begin.

As the military taught me: clarity of mission and shared values turn a group into a team ready for any storm. It readies them to respond to disruption with confidence, from AI or any global uncertainties. I'll never forget the words of **Major General Sir Iain Mackay-Dick KCVO MBE**, my Commanding Officer, as I stood on parade with the 2nd Battalion Scots Guards who were just back from the Falklands War. He looked me in the eye and said:

"You must always prepare for the unexpected!"

That lesson holds true in every boardroom. Prepare your people. Clarify your mission. You'll be ready, no matter what the world throws at you.

YOUR NEXT MISSION

As CEOs, commanders and changemakers, you already know:
Moral Quotient (MQ) and **Purpose Quotient (PQ)** are your anchors. They guide you through complexity and crisis. But here's the truth: you can't lead anyone anywhere if you're running on empty. At the sharp end of leadership, your **Health Quotient (HQ)** is not a side note - it is critical to your mission. Physical energy, mental clarity and emotional steadiness are force multipliers.

No strategy can outrun burnout. No vision will survive if the leader is too exhausted to see the horizon. **Jack Prichard**, CEO of Polyco Healthline, lives this - on the bike, in the gym and in the boardroom. He doesn't just talk about wellbeing; he rode alongside his team in the Inspiring Leadership Foundation's 'Ride to Inspire' charity cycle.
His philosophy is simple:

"Supporting our teams to stay fit and healthy is not just good for business. It's the right thing to do."

Military training taught me this: you are only as strong as your last meal, your last night's rest and your daily discipline. Purpose and integrity steer the ship, but fitness and wellbeing give you the stamina to reach your destination, especially when storms gather.

Before you dive into that endless to-do list, take a breath and use the matrix (opposite). Prioritise what truly matters, go after the important before you chase the urgent, and trust the rest will sort itself out. That discipline is what separates the good from the great.

So, as you turn the page to the next chapter, remember: integrity and purpose set your direction, but your health powers every step. Don't sacrifice it at the altar of ambition. Build the physical strength, balance and habits that let you lead - not just today - but for the long march ahead. Your organisation will only ever be as resilient as you are.

The Prioritisation Matrix

The matrix is divided into four quadrants:

	Urgent	Not Urgent
Important	**Quadrant 1:** Urgent & important *(crises, pressing problems, deadlines).* *"Do it now"*	**Quadrant 2:** Not urgent but important *(planning, prevention, relationship building, learning).* *"Schedule it"*
Not Important	**Quadrant 3:** Urgent but not important *(interruptions, some calls/ emails, some meetings).* *"Delegate it"*	**Quadrant 4:** Not urgent & not important *(busywork, timewasters, trivial tasks).* *"Eliminate it"*

Originally developed by Dwight D. Eisenhower and popularised by Stephen R. Covey in The 7 Habits of Highly Effective People (1989).

40

3
HQ – Health Quotient:
Optimise Your Physical and Mental Performance

What is HQ?

T o lead at the highest level, you must first lead yourself. True performance rests on the daily disciplines:

- Eating well
- Moving often
- Sleeping deeply
- Breathing with intention

Your health is not an afterthought. It's the foundation for sharp thinking, emotional balance, and the energy to inspire those around you. When you make your wellbeing a priority, you give your team permission to do the same. That unlocks reserves of discretionary energy, commitment and creativity - fuel for real business results.

Monitoring Wellbeing

High-performing leaders measure what matters. Make your health one of those metrics. Health technology is revolutionising how we see ourselves. Wearables and apps can now give real-time data on:

- Sleep quality
- Heart rate variability
- Stress and recovery

Soon, they will provide even more - predicting, guiding, prompting action. I have used Fitbit, the Oura ring and now medical-grade Whoop monitors. Whoop MG tells me if I'm performing well verses my biological age (8 years younger), or if I need to adjust.

Yet tech is valuable only if you act on its insights. If you would never ignore a flashing warning on your company dashboard, do not ignore one in your own body. Early detection and action change outcomes. Annual health checks are essential. Neglect can be irreversible. The value lies in listening, adapting, and building stronger routines - without getting obsessive about your data.

Consistent Practices

Top CEOs build their health routine as they build their business: with small, deliberate steps, consistent over time. Leigh and I start many mornings training on our own, or with our personal trainer, **Keegan Bernstein**. This anchors me with clarity, focus and readiness to lead.

Graham Harle, Global CEO of Gleeds (*Podcast 150*), told me:

> *"Endurance cycling keeps me grounded. The discipline I build on the bike translates directly into the resilience and focus I need to lead my business."*

Setting yourself fitness challenges can often spark the motivation needed to prioritise your health. One of my clients, **Sam Mercer**, CEO of Plantforce Rentals (*Podcast 347*) takes competitive health seriously. He competes in HYROX events - high-intensity combinations of cardio, strength and endurance: runs, sledge pushes, functional exercises. Sam is clear on the benefits:

> *"HYROX boosts heart health, muscle strength and endurance - it lifts motivation, improves mental wellbeing and builds community. By the finish, you are whacked but you're elated."*

Whether or not you take on a competitive challenge, remember that small, repeated actions - compounded daily - deliver extraordinary results.

Ask yourself:

"Am I investing daily in my vitality - as much as I invest in my company's growth?"

We live by the "Law of the Harvest". Seeds planted at the last minute rarely yield a bountiful crop. The best leaders invest early and consistently, knowing that steady effort, like sunlight and water, yield results over time.

Discipline

Discipline is the backbone of achievement. The routines you practice shape not just results, but your character. **General David H. Petraeus** (*Podcast 247*), one of the world's most respected military leaders - a four-star U.S. Army General, former Commander in Iraq and Afghanistan, and Director of the CIA - shared this view with me:

> *"Physical fitness is the foundation of mental toughness and disciplined leadership. The habits you build in the gym echo in every boardroom decision you make."*

David's career shows us that strategic vision, clear communication and the ability to inspire teams are amplified by the discipline forged through physical training. The difference between leaders who endure and those who fade lies in mindset.

Scott Parazynski (*Podcast 117*), is a truly extraordinary NASA astronaut, physician and inventor. He flew five Space Shuttle missions, conducted seven spacewalks and became the first person to both fly in space and summit Mount Everest. Scott told me that his success was about:

> *"Consistent, disciplined mental and physical fitness."*

That relentless pursuit of improvement, day by day, was vital in the most demanding environments.

Setting the Pace as a Leader

Yilmaz Erceyes (*Podcast 201*), Chief Marketing Officer and entrepreneur who transformed Premier Foods into a high-performing FTSE 250 company, shared his relentless focus on fitness:

> *"Disciplined fitness is the foundation of my drive and determination in business. Pushing through physical limits teaches me that every challenge, no matter how tough, can be overcome with focus and resilience."*

For Yilmaz, this philosophy shapes his teams. He leads by example, believing leaders who invest in their health inspire their teams to do the same. The habits forged in the gym translate directly into business:

– Set ambitious goals

– Measure progress

– Never settle for mediocrity

This creates a culture where energy, stamina and determination are the norm. **Daniel Bernard** - CEO, investor and entrepreneur (*Podcasts 202 and 303*), invited Leigh and me to join his team to cycle all seven Emirates in seven days, an achievement demanding vision and unity. He told me:

> *"Fitness is my proving ground for leadership. Every mile on the bike is a lesson in discipline, drive and the power of leading from the front."*

For Daniel, the road is both a test and a teacher - where you discover your limits and learn, together, to move beyond them. The greatest leaders are those who inspire others to dig deeper, keep going when it's tough and celebrate every hard-won mile. As you reflect, remember: your drive and discipline, in both fitness and leadership, set the pace for those who follow.

Lead with Grit

Every element of your CEO's Compass is interconnected, but none more so than your Health Quotient - the anchor that energises everything. I learnt much from **Rich Diviney**, former U.S. Navy SEAL Commander (*Podcast 339*), author of *The Attributes* and a pioneer in building elite performance alongside his colleague **Simon Sinek**.

Rich's work shows that true high performance is built not just on skill, but on qualities that endure under pressure. He told me:

> *"In Navy SEAL training, attributes like mental toughness, resilience, and adaptability are the true foundations - more than skills. One recruit struggled with swimming. The instructor said, 'That's fine, we can teach you how to swim.'"*

What mattered was grit and determination. The lesson for your executive team is this: In business, as in life, skills can be taught. But resilience, adaptability and fortitude carry you through crisis.

World-class CEOs deliberately cultivate these inner strengths. When the stakes rise, your true measure is who you are, and how you behave under pressure.

Leadership In Action

Resilience grows when leaders are attuned to the health of their teams. **Dr Ferri Abolhassan**, Board Member Deutsche Telekom AG & CEO T-Systems International GmbH (*Podcast 372*), knows this well. Our coaching sessions take place while running together around a lake. As a former German Parachute Regiment officer and top-level triathlete, his stamina and discipline powers his corporate transformations. His view is clear:

> *"What matters is authenticity, listening to people and maintaining the stamina required to lead large, complex organisations through demanding transformations."*

You can lead your teams with simple, powerful practices:

1. Prioritise self-care to model healthy habits
2. Create a supportive work environment
3. Encourage work-life balance and stress management
4. Foster open, stigma-free conversations about mental health

What world-class leaders do differently is also to:

- **Stay alert** for early signals - nagging pain, low energy, dips in morale
- **Act decisively** - if something's off, investigate it early
- **Make wellbeing a standard** - non-negotiable for everyone
- **Schedule health check-ins** - just like performance reviews

Your Health Quotient is the silent force behind every bold decision, clear strategy and resilient team. Guard it fiercely - for yourself, your people and your future.

Training, Rest and Recovery

Relentless drive deserves respect, but true leaders recognise the power of balance. I am intentional about my training; four sessions a week, avoiding consecutive days. This rhythm safeguards against exhaustion and injury and protects my immune system.

Ignoring recovery leads to fading clarity and poor decision-making. Leaders who neglect rest become vulnerable to illness and lose their edge. This truth was underlined in my conversation with **Anna Hemmings OLY MBE** (*Podcast 6*). Anna, a six-time world champion and double Olympian in marathon kayaking, overcame Chronic Fatigue Syndrome. Her journey warns against overreaching without recovery. She told me:

> *"The old adage 'no pain, no gain' does not make sense, because balancing spending and recovering energy is a fundamental human need. Without adequate recovery, you will compromise your performance, health, energy and wellbeing. I should know - it leads to burnout!"*

World-class performance requires both effort and wisdom. Leaders who master recovery build resilience and sustain performance.

You Are What You Eat

You can't outrun a poor diet. In leadership, as in life, what you fuel yourself with determines your capacity to perform. Our bodies rebuild themselves daily - cell by cell. The quality of what you eat shapes the quality of your thinking, energy and resilience. **Adam Northover**, my personal trainer and a bodybuilding champion, has helped me focus on details that matter:

- Micronutrients
- Real, high-quality food
- How those choices impact performance

His lesson is clear: the leadership decisions you make at work are amplified - or undermined - by choices made in the kitchen.

Be Wary of Shortcuts

The vitamins and supplements industry is immense, offering endless promises. Leaders are often tempted by shortcuts to peak performance, but not all that glitters is gold. Many supplements - even with good intentions - can do harm. I learned this the hard way. For years, I took a cocktail of supplements, only to realise, with the help of a liver specialist, that my liver was under strain. We stripped everything back. Within six weeks, my liver function returned to normal, and my energy and resilience improved.

One supplement does not fit all. If I reintroduce any, it will be with measured testing under medical guidance - one at a time, with blood tests. Now, I focus on:

- Eating clean
- Choosing real food over ultra-processed
- Cutting out added sugars

The result: sharper thinking, better health, improved sleep and renewed wellbeing. If your great-grandparents would not recognise it as food, think twice.

World-Class Standards

Damian McKinney - CEO of DioniLife and founder of the non-alcoholic beer company Mash Gang (*Podcast 382*) - is a serial entrepreneur and former Royal Marine officer. Damian speaks candidly about the scars and victories - and he always champions the highest standards in business and life. He said:

> *"If it's wrong, then it is still wrong. It will always be wrong. Make it right now!"*

Whether in crisis or routine, there is never a right time to ignore what needs fixing. True leaders confront problems immediately. By holding yourself and your team to these standards, you build trust and establish a culture where excellence is the expectation.

Greatness is found in the courage to do what's right - even when difficult.

Sleep Improves Performance

Sleep is the unsung force multiplier in leadership. As **Matthew Walker** reveals in *Why We Sleep*, an extra hour of quality sleep can transform your effectiveness by as much as 30 per cent.

Jamie Waller - serial entrepreneur, author of *The Dyslexic Edge* and a true adventurer (*Podcasts 268 and 342*), has lived this lesson. He has always championed kindness and wellbeing. During one visit, Jamie and I trained with BBC Gladiator **Zach George**. Jamie, open about his struggles with sleep, especially with ADHD, worked relentlessly to improve it. He told me:

> *"For years, I ran on 4 hours of sleep a night and thought I could out-work exhaustion. But real performance, clarity, energy and resilience only came when I made sleep and fitness my non-negotiables."*

For Jamie, prioritising sleep hygiene - creating a restful space, unplugging devices, and using cognitive behavioural techniques - was transformative. For leaders, poor sleep erodes judgement, slows decisions, and undermines resilience.

Personally, health challenges often interrupt my sleep. Now I prioritise a midday power nap. Even brief, deep rest can make a measurable difference. World-class leaders treat sleep and fitness as strategic assets. Prioritise and protect, and you will unlock reserves of clarity and stamina.

Mental Health

In business, what gets measured often matters most. But in mental health, the most vital measures rarely appear on a dashboard. True leaders recognise what you cannot always quantify:

- – The mood of your colleagues
- – The resilience of your teams
- – The wellbeing of your organisation

Professor Sir Cary Cooper (*Podcast 369*), leading authority on mental health, told me:

> *"Wellbeing isn't a luxury for organisations; it's a business imperative. If you do not look after your people, you won't get the best out of them. Mental health is not just the absence of illness. It's about creating environments where people can thrive, feel valued and perform at their best."*

> *"Leaders must recognise that looking after mental health and wellbeing is not just a moral responsibility, but a strategic one. Healthy, happy employees are the foundation of high-performing organisations."*

Measuring mental health is not simple; it demands honest self-reflection and the courage to seek feedback. The strongest leaders spot subtle signs -

a dip in energy, lateness, withdrawal - and rely on restorative habits: breathwork, regular exercise, reflective moments.

Even without precise measurement, you can lead by example. Prioritise your mental health, create space for candid conversations, and foster a culture where strength is found in openness. Leadership brings trials that leave unseen marks. Adversity rarely comes as an isolated event - it arrives as continual pressure, or unexpected loss. I have witnessed even the strongest leaders quietly shaped by stress and trauma.

Through The Inspiring Leadership Foundation, I have seen how trauma ripples outward, touching families and teams. Post-traumatic stress often waits, dormant. It surfaces unexpectedly. Mental health challenges are often hidden; their impact is enduring. Our duty is to create space for these stories, where no one fights alone.

Stress and Psychological Safety

Stress is part of high performance - it sharpens focus. But when it lingers, it erodes resilience and heightens burn-out risk. The warning signs show in your body, your sleep, your relationships. I spoke with **Mandy Hickson** (*Podcast 319*), who was among the first women to fly the RAF Tornado GR4 on the front line. Her journey through pressure and loss is a masterclass in resilience explained in her book: *An Officer, not a Gentleman.*
Mandy told me:

> *"Reflecting on my personal experience of pregnancy loss, it is so important to deal with stress and manage your health. As crazy as it sounds, you can get so busy with work, and I had not realised that I was pregnant and carried on flying initially."*

Leaders must create environments where psychological safety is real - where causes of stress can be identified and addressed early.

Shape a Culture of Trust

As a leader, your responsibility is to shape the culture. Every word, action and silence sets the tone. Culture is forged by your example. As the proverb goes: *"The fish rots from the head."* If your senior team thrives, that is due to your leadership. If they struggle, that too is your signal. Ask yourself:

"What's the real atmosphere in my boardroom? Are people free to challenge, to learn from setbacks - or do they play it safe, waiting for permission?"

The best cultures are built on support, challenge and inspiration. Mistakes are not weapons - they are teachable moments. When setbacks happen, ask:

"What have I learned - and what am I going to do now?"

A culture of blame breeds secrecy and kills growth; a culture of trust and learning fosters innovation and lasting success.

Imagine a workplace where people are free to speak up, be bold, and share mistakes openly. The foundation of psychological safety (another bedrock of good health) is trust, underpinned by collaboration and relentless improvement. Ask yourself:

"What culture am I truly building? Are people flourishing - or merely surviving?"

That answer defines your legacy.

Teamwork and a Shared Purpose

Setting a bold standard for health is more than personal. It sends a message that echoes throughout the organisation. When you put wellbeing and psychological safety first, you create peak performance. Whether training for a marathon or practising mindfulness, your example sets the bar. But it is also about camaraderie and shared achievement. The finish line signals only the beginning - the bond forged is what endures.

As a leader, rally your team to take on challenges that matter: for charity, for community, for excellence.

The ripple effect?

- Stronger bonds
- Shared laughter
- Real accomplishment

When you lead with a high HQ, you change more than your own life; you elevate everyone who follows.

Avoid Workaholism

I once heard a CEO reflect on his career with striking honesty:

"Everything in life is possible - if you're prepared to pay the price and live with the consequences. I achieved great success, but I wonder if the price and the consequences were worth it."

Those words echoed in a candid conversation I had with **Anil Kanti Basu**. We spoke openly about the cost of relentless focus on duty and professional achievement. For him, that cost was personal - the strain on family relationships, the missed moments with his children. His words were sobering:

"I would trade all the medals and newspaper headlines for more time with my children growing up, rather than being such a workaholic. It took me too long to wise up."

The lesson: real leadership is about balance. Drive for results must match a deep deliberate commitment to what matters most - your health, your family, your legacy.

One of the most inspiring leaders I have interviewed was **Al Carns DSO OBE MC MP**, UK Government Veterans and People's Minister, and MP for Birmingham Selly Oak (*Podcast 364*). Al recently led a team of four Special Forces veterans on an extraordinary journey to conquer Mount Everest. Together, they achieved a world record - completing the climb from the UK and back in under seven days. It was a feat of endurance, leadership, and unyielding determination.

His highly decorated Royal Marines and Special Forces career spanned two decades of war in Iraq and Afghanistan. It was a record of service few can match. But when we spoke, this is what Al told me:

"My service to Queen and country involved a total commitment. The price was that, in the 21 years of my daughter's early life, I spent a total of just two years with her. That's a very high price to pay."

As leaders, we must recognise: success is not just measured by what we build - it's also by what we *sustain*. At home. At work. Within ourselves.

Prioritise What Matters Most

There comes a moment - in leadership and life - when you must choose where your presence truly matters. I recall a coaching conversation with **The Rt Hon Dame Tessa Jowell**, not long before her courageous final battle with a brain tumour. Her words cut through the corporate noise:

"Always be where you are indispensable. No one can replace you as parent at a critical moment of your children's life. The meeting you missed - someone else can go in your place."

As CEOs, we are conditioned to be "in the room". Tessa's wisdom reminds us that meetings can wait; moments with loved ones cannot. Lead relentlessly at work, but not at the expense of the moments at home where your leadership is irreplaceable.

Fight for focus at work - fight even harder for presence with your family.

LEADERSHIP WISDOM

Brian Heyworth, CEO and Managing Partner of Lansdowne Partners (*Podcast 147*), is one of the most respected voices in the investment management world. His career has been defined not only by results, but by a willingness to address the difficult conversations - with candour and courage. On my podcast, Brian was refreshingly honest:

> *"It's true. I've spoken very openly about my struggles with alcohol addiction on your podcast. For a long time, I didn't want to talk about it. I was ashamed and felt like I had let people down. But the more I kept it bottled up, the worse it got. I overcame alcohol addiction by seeking help, which I learned is a sign of strength, not weakness."*

> *"Key to my recovery were open conversations about my struggles, prioritising sleep, developing healthy routines and understanding that recovery is a journey. My advice to others is simple, don't be afraid to ask for help. There is hope and support available."*

Brian's story reminds us: true strength is honesty and the courage to reach out. Recovery is built on daily habits, open dialogue, and an unyielding commitment to wellbeing.

YOUR CALL TO ACTION

- Ask yourself: *"Is my culture healthy, or toxic?"* Seek outside perspectives, listen to honest feedback and act to unlock your team's true potential.

- Look after your health as you lead. Is your approach to health as rigorous as your approach to strategy? Tools like Whoop MG offer valuable data; a simple weekly check-in works wonders.

- Pay attention to your mental health. Take time for regular self-assessment and honest conversations. Know that wellbeing is the foundation of high performance.

Your example sets the standard in turbulent times. Daily habits, resilience and openness carry your organisation through any storm.

YOUR NEXT MISSION

The CEOs and executive teams I work with share one trait above all: they treat health and wellbeing as non-negotiable. It is a choice - to lead with energy, clarity and resilience. Your Health Quotient is the fuel for every decision, relationship and inspiration. Put your wellbeing first and signal that high performance starts with healthy leaders. Health is the anchor that steadies your entire compass.

Invest in yourself. You'll find the capacity to lead with empathy, clarity, and conviction. Next, we turn to the **Emotional Quotient (EQ)** - the skill that sets great leaders apart. EQ is your secret weapon for reading the room, building trust, and leading through uncertainty. Exceptional leaders who use their emotional and social skills with the same precision they bring to the boardroom, recognise that true distinction comes not only from what you know, but from how you connect.

Remember: health and emotional intelligence are not luxuries. They are essentials for navigating today's complexity and leaving a legacy that endures.

4
EQ – Emotional & Social Quotient:
Build Connection and Rapport

What is EQ?

To use your emotions and social skills intelligently as a leader, you must:

- Be aware of and understand your emotions and express them appropriately
- Relate well to others by understanding their feelings and perspectives
- Manage and control your emotions to handle daily demands, challenges and pressures
- Adapt to change and solve personal and interpersonal problems with composure
- Generate a positive mood to stay motivated and fully engaged

EQ is often described as a set of *"soft skills"*. This can create the illusion that these abilities are somehow less valuable than *"hard"* technical skills, that they are innate, or that they cannot be measured. None of this stands up to scrutiny. It's the reason many now refer to them as *"power skills"*.

Emotional mastery is the foundation of world-class leadership. Like any vital skill, it can be learned and measured. One of the ways to do this is with the Inspiring Leadership Compass framework, built from decades of practical experience and research into what enables high-performing leaders and teams.

Centred on a set of measurable quotients, the Compass allows you to assess your strengths and areas for development through the *ILI Self-report*, *ILI Team report* and *ILI 360-degree feedback*. This clarity enables you to focus your growth, ensuring your leadership remains intentional and effective. Investing in EQ unlocks your capacity for clarity, compassion and meaningful impact.

A Personal Story - The Importance of EQ

After two years at Staff College and commanding my company on operations in Northern Ireland and Bosnia, I had been selected for the job I had always wanted: Chief of Staff, 15 (North East) Brigade.

Yet I felt forced to resign.

That bleak moment stays with me. I can still picture the dark wooden role of honour board with names in gold lettering. Most were future generals and brigadiers - decorated, celebrated, highly capable. Next to those names I felt out of my depth, unworthy, and overwhelmed by responsibility. My only solution, I thought, was a sideways move to somewhere easier.

The real issue? I lacked emotional and social intelligence. I wasn't reading the environment, nor my colleagues, accurately. I missed the mood in Brigade HQ and the wider command: my team wanted connection and opportunities to grow. Yet when they brought me problems, I replied:

"Leave it with me."
"I'll have a think about that."

I was trying too hard to impress, rather than connect. I wrongly thought that the key to success was proving my independent capability. Yet my leadership had become *transactional*, rather than *relational*.

The idiom of "monkey on my back" has its roots in the world of heroin addiction. Not sure you want to have that underlying meaning here that some might read into. A potential better idiom would be "millstone around my neck".

Metaphorically, the problem, or "millstone", each colleague arrived with would then be placed around my neck. My Chief of Staff's office was soon full of these millstones. Heavier problems kept coming and my workload was growing. I wrongly cast myself as the superhero by believing I should solve everyone's problems. I didn't even have a *"To Stop Doing"* list. Big mistake.

CEOs should remember **Rear Admiral Grace Hopper's** sharp distinction:

> *"You manage things; you lead people."*

Simon Sinek reinforces this crucial mindset shift - true leadership is not about simply *"being in charge"*, but about *being responsible for the people in your charge*.

The Turning Point - The Coach Approach

On the edge of resignation, I received wise counsel from a retired officer who advocated *"the coach approach to leadership"*. Through his mentoring, I learned: the breakthrough does not come from working longer hours, or greater sacrifice. It comes from developing emotional intelligence:

- Listening deeply, resisting interruption
- Giving people space to think for themselves
- Holding back your solution so they can find their own

This approach requires patience, humility and discipline.

The Power of Great Questions

John C. Maxwell, in *Good Leaders Ask Great Questions*, champions inquiry as central to leadership. He writes:

> *"Good leaders ask great questions that inspire others to dream more, think more, learn more, do more, and become more."*

His message is clear. The right questions spark growth and innovation. When a team member claims, *"I can't do that - it's too difficult,"* do not take back their task. Instead, ask: *"If you could do it, how might you?"* Hypotheticals encourage creativity and courage, smashing limiting beliefs. This is about shaping the environment, so the team grows in capability.

Sir Ken Robinson teaches that leaders:

"Germinate seeds of possibility and draw on people's talents, helping them find their element and build a high-trust environment."

Expect people to solve their own problems - then they will start to believe it too. Upwards delegation stops. Millstones return to their rightful owners.

The TGROW Coaching Model in Action

Kevin Roberts, renowned figure in the advertising world, having revolutionised brand marketing with his concept of "Lovemarks" and as CEO of Saatchi & Saatchi (*Podcast 108*), shared his view that:

"Leadership is about igniting the fire within others, not dictating their path. Help them discover their potential and guide them to become the best versions of themselves."

This avoids dependency and *"learned helplessness"*. Inspiring leaders motivate teams to maximise their own potential. When our Brigade Chief Financial Officer arrived stressed and anxious, I used the TGROW Coaching Model:

- **Topic:** What is this really about?
- **Goal:** What do you want to achieve - in the next five minutes?
- **Reality:** What are the facts - succinctly?
- **Options:** What three options do you have?
- **Will to act:** What have you learned, and what will you do now?

By asking, reallocating, and empowering, my workload became manageable, and my team grew stronger. When our Brigade HQ had the chance to lead a mission to Australia for UN Operations - to prevent the East Timor massacre - we could go, knowing the home team performed flawlessly. Even there, the coach approach transformed our work with Allied partners.

That earned me a place in my Brigadier's citation, and an MBE from Queen Elizabeth II. EQ delivers results and builds teams for tomorrow's challenges.

The EQ Impact

Decades of work with CEOs have shown me it's rarely IQ that sustains a leader; it is EQ. **Daniel Goleman** and the Centre for Creative Leadership confirm that EQ accounts for more than half the factors driving leadership success, far outweighing IQ alone.

Brian J. Esposito, CEO and Founder of Esposito Intellectual Enterprises (*Podcasts 174, 264 and 389*), leads across 25 industries, 150 joint ventures, and is a two-time top 10 CEO. He puts it plainly:

"Emotional intelligence is the cornerstone of effective leadership. If you have a good heart and care about others, you can resolve any conflict rationally."

Admiral Mike Manazir (*Podcast 270*), is a Top Gun pilot, inspirational commander of the USS Nimitz aircraft carrier and author of *Learn How to Lead to Win*. He shared that without emotionally intelligent leadership, psychological safety can be impacted, limiting innovation and growth:

"Lead from the heart, not the title. When human connection is absent, people will fear failure, so they won't try, won't take risks and won't bring their full potential."

Gary C. Laney (*Podcast 175*) is a celebrated CEO, bestselling author of *The Power of Strategic Influence* and thought leader whose career has been defined by his extraordinary ability to build powerful networks and foster authentic relationships. He told me:

"Relationships are the currency of business. The stronger your connections, the greater your influence and impact."

Success is not about collecting contacts - it's about building high-value relationships through trust, generosity, and genuine intention.

Three Essential EQ Radars

Inspiring leaders master these three essential radars:

1. **Self-awareness**: tuning in to your emotions and understanding how they shape your actions and decisions.

2. **Empathy**: reading those around you; discerning their needs, motivations and the subtle shifts in mood that can make or break a team's performance.

3. **Organisational awareness**: stepping back to sense the broader culture, picking up on what's happening beneath the surface and anticipating challenges, before they arise.

Elke Anderl, Chief Commercial Officer of T-Systems International (*Podcast 386*), exemplifies this approach. She has a gift for building deep trust and lasting business relationships - even in the demanding, fast-paced world of technology. She understands that true achievement isn't measured by transactions, but by turning customers into loyal advocates and genuine fans. Elke told me:

> *"Business relationships are built on trust and mutual respect. When you focus on understanding your customers and put their needs at the heart of every decision, you don't just earn their loyalty. You turn them into passionate advocates for your brand."*

Every customer interaction is a chance to build trust and deepen value. The strongest leaders listen deeply and act with integrity. **Jonny Gray**, first CEO of the International Tennis Integrity Agency and now with multiple Non-Executive Director (NED) roles (*Podcast 14*), told me:

> *"Take the time to understand people and their motivations. Everybody has a different incentive. What motivates people? What do they need from their leader? How can you help them to be successful? Those, for me, were the key attributes I learned."*

World-class leaders do not just manage tasks - they read people, situations, and themselves with precision.

Be an Expert Listener

One of a leader's greatest assets is the ability to truly read people. To sense the subtle shifts in mood, in motivation, in intent - the undercurrents that so often decide the difference between success and failure. The best leaders don't just hear what is said. They listen for what is beneath the surface, what is unsaid - reading the room, noticing the smallest signals and responding with precision.

Roland Rudd, Founder and Chairman of FGS Global (*Podcast 312*), is a master of strategic communications - advising a quarter of the FTSE 100 and guiding companies with wise counsel through their most critical moments. He told me:

> *"Building strong relationships is at the core of effective leadership. Communication isn't just about what you say. It's about how you listen, how you connect and how you earn trust."*

Authentic leadership is rooted in curiosity, not just communication. Trust is built in quiet moments of true connection. **Huw Owen**, highly respected leader and CEO of Ark Data Centres (*Podcast 166*) was shaped by his service in the Royal Hong Kong Police and cautions:

> *"Many leaders think they are great listeners. Inspiring leaders must listen deeply, even when they think that they have already decided. Explaining decisions and making people feel heard is crucial for engagement."*

To lead well, you must listen well. When you listen - really listen - you create space where others feel valued and empowered.

Build Something Others Want to Be Part of

Craig Hatch, President of Tetra Tech Europe (*Podcast 254*), embodies the kind of leadership that quietly transforms organisations from within. His approach is rooted in humility, humanity and an unwavering commitment to making a real difference. Not through bravado - but through genuine emotional intelligence and deep respect for those he leads. Craig put it simply:

"Leadership is about listening first and acting with empathy. When you truly understand your people, you can help them achieve more than they ever thought possible."

It is no surprise that **Danny Payne**, former CEO of the Foreign and Commonwealth Services and an inspiring leader in his own right (*Podcast 54*), chose to work alongside Craig. That speaks volumes: top talent is drawn to leaders who can truly understand the perspectives and ambitions of their people, and guide them to unlock full potential.

Focus on Self-Improvement

World-class leaders also look inward - measuring success by character and consistent action. Criticism, even when sharp, becomes a tool for growth. **Marcus Aurelius** wrote:

"If anyone can refute me, show me I'm making a mistake or looking at things from the wrong perspective, I'll gladly change it. It's the truth I'm after, and the truth never harmed anyone."

Each challenge, each uncomfortable truth, is an invitation to refine leadership. **Major General Andrew Mackay CBE** (*Podcast 181*), co-founder of Complexas and former coalition commander in Afghanistan, told me:

"One of the most important aspects of EQ is candour. There are ways that you can be honest without being confrontational, and there are ways that you can be candid without being judgmental, or trying to belittle."

"It is an absolutely essential component of successful leadership. When you're having to break bad news to someone: 'You're not getting that promotion' or 'It's your work that needs to improve', you must not fudge it. Those are very difficult conversations and

they can be painful for both sides. The key is that it is always better afterwards."

His words urge us to seek truth, embrace candour, and use every difficulty as a springboard for growth.

The Parable of the Three Envelopes

It is tempting for CEOs to deflect blame. There is a classic parable that illustrates this. A new CEO finds three numbered envelopes from their predecessor with a note: *"Open these during a crisis."*

Six months in, trouble hits. He opens Envelope 1: *"Blame your predecessor."* He does exactly that and buys himself time.

Six months later, another crisis. He opens Envelope 2: *"Blame your team and reorganise."* He restructures, but the core problems remain.

A year later, with the company still faltering, he opens Envelope 3. It reads: *"Prepare three envelopes for your successor."*

Emotionally intelligent leadership is about ownership, confronting the real issues, and building lasting solutions. This takes candour and courage.

Deanna Oppenheimer (*Podcast 80*) also shared wisdom on this theme. A former CEO of Barclays Retail Bank, Deanna is a renowned global corporate leader who has held pivotal roles, transforming institutions into customer-centric champions. Her career includes senior leadership at companies such as Tesco, Tesco Bank, and Intercontinental Hotels Group. She told me:

"Leadership is fundamentally about people. Don't avoid the difficult honest conversations. Early in my career, I learned a valuable lesson that direct and compassionate management of performance challenges is crucial. By embracing this approach, leaders can empower their teams to grow, overcome obstacles and achieve their full potential."

Confront issues early and fully, with compassion and candour, to drive collective high-performance.

LEADERSHIP WISDOM

General Sir Rupert Smith KCB DSO & Bar OBE QGM is a leader whose career has shaped modern strategy at the highest level (*Podcast 94*). He has guided multinational forces through the most complex operations of our time, from the Gulf War to Northern Ireland. He shared wisdom on leadership and command:

"Those we command have to have the confidence and the trust in themselves that they know where they're going. They trust that the commander will look after them on the way. Your role as a commander is having to create a situation where those you are commanding have that degree of self-trust that they can do it. And that's the difference between the two - leadership and command. And I think the breakpoint, very, very roughly, is around 100 people."

"My reason for that is that you can stand up amongst 100 people, they can all see you, you can talk to them, you can remember all their names, and so forth. So, you can have that relationship where they trust you. The moment you are a commander, you have to work a different trick altogether, which is to get those people to have faith in themselves."

This insight highlights a pivotal transition as people move from direct personal engagement to strategic leadership positions. The emphasis shifts from being trusted by others to cultivating trust and confidence within them. Ultimately, both effective command and inspired leadership depend on strong people skills: the ability to build relationships, instil confidence, and empower those you lead to trust both themselves and the vision ahead.

YOUR CALL TO ACTION

- **How effective is your listening?** Do you find your attention wandering or are you truly present? If you are bold, ask your team to rate you from 1 to 10.

- **Practise summarising what your team has said**.
  Try PLAY – REPLAY – OK:
    Play = Let them speak
    Replay = Summarise what you heard
    OK? = Check you have it right, so they feel heard

- **Pick a reality TV programme** and watch it with a team member known for EQ. Mute the sound and study the body language. Note the emotions. Then replay with the sound on - see what you missed. This sharpens your skill at reading unspoken cues.

YOUR NEXT MISSION

In military command and in the boardroom, no leader wins alone. EQ lets you read the room; **Collective and Cultural Intelligence (CQ)** gives you the power to unite it. The next leadership chapter is about forging connections across background, belief, and perspective, turning diversity into your greatest advantage.

Mark Leppard MBE, Headmaster of The British School Al Khubairat and Chairman of British Schools of the Middle East (*Podcast 194*), embodies this. He orchestrates a symphony of different voices, not by cloning himself but by assembling teams where students, staff, and parents all strive for greatness. He teaches:

> *"Collective and cultural intelligence is what sets exceptional leaders and teams apart. It's the ability to work seamlessly with groups from a wide range of backgrounds, harnessing diverse perspectives to drive better decision-making and innovation."*

This is not just tolerance - it is active engagement. Great leaders seek and nurture difference, so critical decisions are shaped by the broadest wisdom. Their legacy is respect, inclusion, and shared achievement - a culture where each person brings their best. Take a moment to ask yourself:

"Am I nurturing a monoculture, or building a mosaic? Am I inspiring a team to challenge, elevate, and achieve more together than any single leader ever could?"

World-class leadership is never a solo act. Its true power lies in the collective, and in the culture you craft and leave behind. Now, unlock the full potential of your own organisation.

"It's amazing what you can achieve if you don't care who gets the credit."

Attributed to Harry Truman

70

5
CQ: Collective & Cultural Quotient:
Drive Cognitive Diversity

What is CQ?

Collective and cultural intelligence distinguishes exceptional leaders and teams. It is the skill to work seamlessly across backgrounds and viewpoints, harnessing diverse perspectives to drive sharper innovation and better decision-making.

With high CQ you do not just tolerate difference - you actively seek it out. You delegate wisely and elevate collective performance by ensuring every voice gets heard, especially those unlike your own. This is how lasting teams outperform the sum of their parts.

A Personal Story - "So, Which School Did You Go To?"

That question, asked by my fellow Officer James, was a ritual. There were three of us - platoon Captains from different regiments - in one office. James, from the Grenadier Guards, always began interviews for his regiment the same way:

"So, which school did you go to?"

The words might be delivered with a smile, but they were a test. Did you belong in his world? Did you fit his mould? Rob and I would tease him about his bias for Eton and Harrow. Comedy wrapped around real truth.

Then, and sometimes still now, the *"right"* school - and a private income - mattered. Years of watching recruitment cycles taught me how easily leaders fall into hiring versions of themselves. The familiar feels safe, but that comfort has a cost. Only hiring *"people like you"* risks groupthink and stifles the creative spark your business needs.

The Power of Difference

I have seen, time and again, that the most successful executive teams are mosaics built from:

- Different roles
- Different lived experiences
- Different motivations
- Different decision-making instincts

If you want extraordinary results, resist cloning yourself. Build a patchwork of perspectives and encourage voices that challenge you. This is not theory - it is proven business practice.

Covering Each Other's Weaknesses

Oz Alashe MBE, CEO and Founder of CybSafe (*Podcast 324*), bridges behavioural science, data analytics, and frontline Special Forces service. His life's work focuses on making society safer by managing human cyber risk and building cultures of trust. Oz told me:

> *"I've learned to work with people who are very different to me. If you bring in people who are just like you, then all you've got is a whole bunch of your weaknesses being magnified. If you bring in people who are different to you, then your weaknesses are covered by their strengths and vice versa."*

Diversity is not just a safeguard; it is the engine for value that exceeds any individual's limits.

The Business Advantage

Our *ILI Inspiring Leadership Inventory* and *ILI 360° Feedback* tools often reveal teams rich in diversity deliver the highest engagement and performance.

The world's top-performing companies know cognitive diversity is not a luxury. It is a strategic necessity. **John Browett**, Chair of the Institute of Directors, is a passionate advocate for equality and inclusion (*Podcast 330*).

He has built his leadership legacy on the belief that diverse teams drive the best results.

John's career speaks for itself: CEO of Dunelm, Dixons and Monsoon Accessorize. Senior leadership roles at Apple and Tesco. Chair of Octopus Group. He has led transformative change; always championing openness, representation and bringing in talent from every walk of life. He reinforced this message, telling me:

"When you bring people together with different backgrounds, perspectives and experiences, you unlock creativity, resilience and better decision-making. As leaders, our responsibility is to seek out that diversity in the talent we hire and to create a culture where everyone feels they truly belong and can thrive."

For John, inclusion is not only moral, but it also makes commercial sense. Make diversity the heart of your culture and two things happen: you attract the best, and you build nimble teams equipped for change.

Ankur Sinha, Chief Product and Technology Officer at Remitly Global (*Podcast 231*), has led teams at Microsoft and Google. He's proven himself not only through technical mastery but also the unwavering belief in the power of diversity to drive innovation. Ankur told me:

"The best teams aren't built on sameness. They thrive on the strengths that come from different backgrounds and experiences. When you bring together people with unique perspectives, you spark innovation that simply can't be achieved any other way."

It is openness to difference that sets your team apart. Real breakthroughs come when leaders seek diverse views, respect others, and empower everyone to contribute.

The Role of Environment in Driving Inclusion

Real performance goes beyond diversity on a spreadsheet. John and Ankur both highlight the need to create environments where every person feels mentally safe to contribute. The best leaders intentionally grow cultural intelligence and trust, crafting a climate where everyone feels valued.

Chris Silcock, MD of Kellanova UK & Ireland (*Podcast 395*), has an extensive leadership career, spanning senior roles at Kellogg's, Coca-Cola European Partners, and Asda. Having worked with Chris, I respect him deeply for his commitment to team empowerment and growth. Chris describes this perfectly:

> *"It's key to listen to and truly hear those you lead. I've come to realise the privilege of my position is to draw from the expertise of others. If I fully empower them to be better in their roles, then I've done my job. They trust me to trust them."*

Bruce Lyman, a globally experienced CEO whose journey spans government, private sector and not-for-profit leadership (*Podcast 218*), concurs. A Royal Australian Air Force veteran, he has built teams from the ground up in some of the world's most demanding environments: Afghanistan, Yemen, Saudi Arabia, China and beyond.

His tip is to: *delegate to the point of discomfort.* Bruce told me:

> *"All the successes that I've had and the massive growth I've experienced - it is because we were able to attract some really wonderful, incredible people and empower them to grow it. The number one thing for me is that it's not all about me. It's all about the diversity of your team."*

Your job is to engineer an environment where diversity is tangible, where every voice matters, where teams own their goals and are equipped for what comes next.

David Heron (*Podcast 23*), Group CEO of Wilton & Bain, is known for championing teamwork over ego, and for transforming businesses through a culture of generosity, reciprocity and accountability. David aims to move beyond the force of personality and personal agenda:

> *"Mis-leaders and expiring leaders suck the life out of you and create a 'not invented here' environment. Success is rarely about one great man or woman."*

The worst leaders sap life from others and wall themselves off. To harness diversity, do not command alone from the front. Instead, foster an environment where people feel confident to challenge and collaborate.

Your Army of Giants

Nando Cesarone (*Podcast 204*), President of U.S. Operations at UPS, climbed from part-time handler to President of UPS's largest division. He distilled his experience:

> *"I firmly believe that you can't manage every single idea in a company from just one office. That's why it is so important to build a strong network of people who are, frankly, much smarter than you are."*

Creating an *"army of giants"* means decentralising leadership. Trust your talented people. Give them space and authority. Engagement thrives at every level. Nando advises:

> *"Surround yourself with smart people and give them the authority to act. When you trust your team and empower them, extraordinary things happen."*

Greatness grows with others, never alone. Leadership is built with giants - those you uplift, trust and inspire to reach higher together.

Spotting and Nurturing Hidden Talent

Steven Cooper CBE, CEO of Aldermore Group and Chair of Experian UK (*Podcast 259*), has built his career on a simple truth: the best teams are forged from the *overlooked*, not the *obvious*. From starting as a bank teller, Steven rose through the ranks at Barclays to CEO roles at C. Hoare & Co. and now Aldermore Bank. He champions social mobility, diversity, and inclusion; not as buzzwords, but as daily, lived leadership. Steven told me:

"In my experience, some of the best talent, particularly talent that develops over time, comes from less obvious places. The challenge is how to find that talent in the first place and then to nurture it to ensure potential is fulfilled."

High performance means identifying and investing in overlooked people - regardless of background or accent. Real inclusion is a lived practice, not just a leadership value.

If building a world-class team is your aim: ensure equal opportunity, set the standard, and make finding hidden talent your business and your legacy.

When You Build Diversity, You Build Resilience

A team that reflects only the obvious will be outpaced by one that includes and develops overlooked talent. Diversity does not just tick boxes. It builds deep resilience, high performance, and an organisation ready for change.

Pavita Cooper, Chair of the 30% Club, experienced NED and former Commissioner for the Equality and Human Rights Commission (*Podcast 345*) devotes her career to highlighting and correcting inequality - especially for women. She has guided change in global boardrooms:

"Companies with women at senior levels responded better to the 2008 financial crisis and the pandemic. When companies go through difficult times, having more women on boards positively affects how decisions are made and the quality of the decisions."

For Pavita, equity is not only fairness, but also the foundation for resilient organisations. Her demand is clear: do not just talk diversity. Measure, track and account for it.

Be Rigorous

Harry Matovu KC is a trailblazing King's Counsel and one of the UK's foremost commercial barristers (*Podcast 224*). As Founder and Chair of the Black Talent Charter, Harry has united leading law firms, financial institutions and professional services - alongside the UK Supreme Court - in a transformative coalition to open doors and build lasting pipelines of black talent from entry-level to senior leadership. Harry told me:

> *"Sydney Kentridge, a barrister who defended Nelson Mandela and Steve Biko's family, showed me that true leadership means speaking truth to power, even at personal cost. His moral courage inspired me to champion the Black Talent Charter, which addresses workplace racial disparity. I learned that leadership isn't about personal gain, but about using one's voice to advocate for what's right and drive meaningful change in society."*

In his work to address the deep-rooted misperceptions of black talent in business and the professions, he challenges the lack of rigour that is applied to inclusion. Inclusion cannot be enacted by good intentions alone. As well as measurable action, he says that true inclusion demands brave leadership and a willingness from majority groups to create genuinely welcoming environments.

Harry believes that progress is only possible when organisations apply the same rigour to diversity and inclusion as they do to business growth. Leaders need to have the humility and courage to face uncomfortable truths and build a future where talent is recognised on a level playing field.

His legacy is a call to action; to move beyond words, build real pipelines of opportunity and ensure that every talented individual can see themselves reflected at the very top.

Speak Up

Bias, both subtle and overt, persists in every industry. Two of my closest friends, Errol from Jamaica and Himalaya from Nepal, faced exclusion at Sandhurst. Not always in words - in the missed invitations, the knowing glances, the feeling of difference. We have spoken about those experiences. At the time, I'd challenge some bias but too often was silent - believing it was not my place. That silence, the bystander effect, is complicity.

Silence gives approval to behaviour with no place in a high-performing culture. The burden of challenging bias must not fall only on those most affected. Errol, usually calm, nearly lost it when faced with direct racism. Even the strongest can be ground down by the thousand cuts of prejudice.

Interrogate your own organisation. Where might bias slip in? Are you hiring and promoting "Mini-Mes" or encouraging a truly inclusive culture? Ask yourself:

"Do I challenge bad behaviour or let it pass? Have I ever been the silent bystander?"

Evil, as history reminds us, thrives when good people do nothing.

LEADERSHIP WISDOM

Mark Urban is a distinguished British journalist, historian and broadcaster (*Podcast 370*); renowned for his fearless commitment to truth and his deep knowledge of defence, foreign affairs and military history. From the moment he stepped into the newsroom, he stood out. As a founding Defence Correspondent for *The Independent* and later as Diplomatic Editor for almost three decades on BBC's *Newsnight*, he built a reputation for incisive intelligence and fearless enquiry.

His military background shaped him. It gave him discipline, precision, and a clear-eyed commitment to integrity; values he carried into every aspect of his journalism.

Mark became known for challenging authority and exposing lies. His investigative work tackled some highly sensitive subjects. During his time at *Newsnight*, Mark was celebrated for incisive questioning and his refusal to accept cover-ups or misinformation. He led by example - guiding his team to dig deeper and ask the questions others avoided. Reflecting on his approach, Mark said:

> *"You have to look at the facts and challenge the lies, no matter who is telling them. Journalism, like leadership, is about holding power to account and making sure the truth comes out, even when it's uncomfortable or inconvenient."*

YOUR CALL TO ACTION

1. Embrace Difference

Ask yourself:
"How open am I to people with different viewpoints?"

Rate this from 1 to 10. Then invite honest, anonymous feedback from at least ten colleagues. This search for blind spots opens the door to more diverse thinking in your team. *Harvard Business Review* (2019) cites that when employees feel they belong, job performance rises 56%, turnover halves, and sick days drop.

2. Turn Insight Into Action

Review your latest 360° Feedback. How closely does your self-view match what colleagues see? What will you do differently this week to show your willingness to adapt?

3. Lead With Courage

Think back - when did you last challenge unacceptable behaviour, especially when someone "different" was targeted? Make it your mission to speak up this week - at meetings, in the corridor, or even in moments of subtle exclusion. Courage grows stronger every time you use it.

4. The 21-Day No Complaints Challenge

Encourage your team to try 21 days without complaints or gossip. Use a coloured bracelet as a daily reminder. The goal is progress, not perfection. This reframes mindsets from spotting problems to seeking solutions.

5. Pay It Forward

This week, look for two opportunities to help strangers with small acts of kindness. Encourage your team to do the same. Ask those you help to pay it forward, rippling generosity throughout your organisation.

Your example sets the tone for your team. Embrace difference, act on feedback, lead with courage, cultivate positivity and build a legacy that inspires people to follow.

YOUR NEXT MISSION

The journey to greatness is never a solo march. CQ is not just about diversity for appearance's sake - it is the steel in your organisation's spine when the headwinds come. True CQ means encouraging each unique voice - building teams with depth, adaptability and trust that endure any storm.

Anthony 'Staz' Stazicker, recipient of the *Conspicuous Gallantry Cross* (CGC), is living proof (*Podcast 396*). Orphaned at eleven. Bullied. Denied his dream of a football career through injury. Yet he rose; not just to serve in Tier 1 SBS elite forces, but to earn one of gallantry's highest honours and thrive as an entrepreneur, standing atop Mount Everest.

Staz embodies resilience. He turned hardship into a launchpad, using discipline and determination to outfight the odds. Most importantly, Staz exemplifies the power of CQ. By drawing on diverse perspectives, backgrounds, and ideas, he builds teams that are both adaptable and resilient. His message to business leaders is as sharp as simple: Reframe disaster. Nurture powerful habits. Never go it alone. Build a team whose grit matches your own; the kind exemplified through his recent record-breaking Everest ascent.

Remember: it is your connections and culture that make you unbreakable. Ahead is the **Resilience Quotient** (RQ) - your toolkit for overcoming the storms you know are coming. Ask yourself:

"Does my culture - my collective - lift me when I falter and double my courage when the challenge hits?"

Because true leadership shines brightest, not in calm waters, but when adversity demands unity, trust and resolve. Defeat is often optional and can be avoided by those who prepare.

6
RQ - Resilience Quotient:
Thrive in Adversity

What is RQ?

Resilience is your ability to face disappointment, crisis, or even catastrophe and come back wiser, stronger and more agile than before. It is not just about being tough or unfeeling. Nor is it a simplistic ability to bounce back. Real resilience is about becoming anti-fragile, so that the blows of life do not just leave you standing - they sharpen your edge.

With the discipline to reflect, adapt, and grow, obstacles become stepping stones towards greater wisdom and capability. Embracing an "OMMS" mindset (Obstacles Make Me Stronger) does not mean ignoring pain or vulnerability. Pain and vulnerability become the raw material for growth. Leaders with high resilience recognise that vulnerability is not weakness. It is the wellspring of courage, and of deeper human connection.

A Personal Story - The Leap

In both business and life, there are moments when hesitation is costly.

I saw this during selection for P Company - the gruelling entrance to the UK Airborne Forces. Over four and a half days, you face eight physical and mental tests: loaded marches, assault courses, and milling - boxing under pressure. Those who pass wear the maroon beret and parachute wings, the symbol of elite airborne soldiers.

I was 60 feet up, preparing to leap across a yawning gap.

My knees were shaking. I had no harness. Just a Para helmet - and a choice.

"Standby!" the Airborne instructor bellowed.

The scaffolding plank seemed impossibly far. I could either leap, or let doubt win.

Two soldiers before me hadn't made it. They'd frozen, trapped by over-thinking, replaying worst case scenarios until fear became self-fulfilling. They'd climbed down. Packed their kit away. Their dreams over.

Leadership is forged in moments when fear, adrenaline and decision collide.

I forced my focus, blocked out the chaos, launched with surging adrenaline - and made it. The greatest risk is often letting fear dictate your actions.

The best leaders I coach know: resilience is built on decisive action in testing moments, not endless rumination.

Small Steps

Some people say I'm too driven, even obsessive. Perhaps so. Yet, when challenges threaten to overwhelm, focus is your greatest ally. Break adversity into manageable compartments.

Think only ten minutes ahead, then repeat, again and again.

I learned that in Long Valley, during my Airborne selection, on an infamous, 10-mile march through ankle-deep mud and water, under relentless pressure. As an officer, you lead from the front. You motivate. You never leave anyone behind.

When Private Jenkins fell 300 meters back, I went back for him. Helping him forward with encouragement, our instructor, Corporal Snatch, tested my leadership further. He barked:

"Now, Sir... you carry Jenkins' pack..."

Leadership is action, not words. Snatch's methods - doubling my load, constant criticism - were brutal, but revealing.

He continued:

"Just admit it, Sir… you're a loser. Give up. You're not good enough to be an Airborne Officer. Quit now… Just get on the wagon and go back to your unit..."

Ten minutes. That was all I could allow myself to think about under Snatch's barrage. In the distance, the Land Rover engine revved, waiting for the quitters.

Resilience is built in the chaos, not in the comfort. So I narrowed my focus: just one foot in front of the other.

When Jenkins was called back for his pack, I re-joined the squad - barely able to speak - but I kept going.

This is what inspiring leaders do: they compartmentalise, keep moving, and lead by example, especially under scrutiny. That refusal to quit, more than any speech, earns trust.

A Modern Parallel - Reinventing Yourself

Martin Dougherty, COO of NIAB and former Executive at the Wellcome Sanger Institute (*Podcast 69*), lives by lifelong learning. Never content to stand still, he set himself the challenge of transforming his health and became a competitive bodybuilder. Martin told me:

> *"Resilience is not about never falling down. It's about getting back up, every single time, with more purpose and focus than before. Determination is choosing to keep moving forward, even when progress feels slow and the odds seem stacked against you."*

Martin's story underlines this truth: a commitment to continuous improvement and unyielding determination will set you - and your team - apart.

Expect the Unexpected and Dig Deep

Leadership demands readiness for shifting conditions.

I remember one morning in Airborne Selection: we crested a hill, hungry, and saw Army chefs with full breakfasts on pristine tablecloths. For a moment, it seemed the reward had come. Then the chief instructor's voice rang out:

"These are not for you. You do not deserve it. Keep going."

He kicked over the table, food flew. Some soldiers quit at once, bitter at the unfairness. The Sergeant was unmoved:

"The enemy does not play fair. Setbacks happen. What you want will not always arrive."

The world owes you no comfort.

In business, as in life, setbacks will come at the worst moments. The best leaders keep going when disappointment threatens their spirit. They dig deep, adapt, and lead on, even when the reward is snatched away.

So, when a deal collapses, markets shift, or recognition is denied, remember: resilience is forged in your response when the rug is pulled out from under you. That response earns your team's trust and the right to lead them forward.

Build Your Reserves

In business, setbacks are inevitable. World-class leaders know resilience is not built in the moment you need it; it is built every day. It lives in the habits, the mindset and the culture you shape long before the storm arrives. They prepare their teams to absorb impact and keep moving, no matter how many times they have to start over.

Archie Norman, Chairman of Marks & Spencer, is a master of resilience and turnarounds (*Podcast 338*). With a career leading giants like Asda and ITV, and a track record of guiding businesses through turbulence, his leadership is defined by calm under pressure and the ability to draw on reserves when it matters most. Archie told me:

> *"After nearly 7 years, the change has been slow, but I do think with the executive team we have under Stuart's leadership, we are on a path that will be irreversible. We are creating the M&S as it should be for the next 100 years. I don't think leadership can be bottled into a phrase. I think my top tip to people in leadership is: Be humble. Listen first. Live the values. Work hard."*

Archie's words capture the heart of RQ. True resilience lies not in quick fixes, but in humility, perseverance and the daily commitment to rebuild and adapt, regardless of the obstacles. Resilient leaders model steady resolve, guiding their teams forward - especially in times of uncertainty. This kind of steady resilience is the bridge to what comes next.

Turn Setbacks Into Strength

Adversity reveals a leader's true character. I have seen it in myself and in the CEOs and teams I have coached. The obstacle is a proving ground for reinvention and self-discovery. Face challenges with grit, and setbacks become lessons for something greater. This is your *hero's journey* - facing fear, surmounting obstacles and coming back wiser. Ask yourself:

"What story am I living? What obstacles stand in my way? Most importantly; how will I choose to respond?"

Every challenge is a chance to inspire and grow, raising up those you lead. **Gavin Patterson**, former Global CEO of BT and Chief Revenue Officer of Salesforce (*Podcast 305*), built his career on driving transformation and innovation, even when the stakes were high. He has never avoided tough calls and told me:

> *"You learn far more from your setbacks than your successes. Every time something didn't go to plan, it forced me to reflect, adapt and come back stronger."*

He also spoke about the importance of humility, self-reflection and the courage to take risks, even when the outcome was far from certain.

Cath Possamai, Talent Acquisition Director for Amazon, leads 1,500 recruiters, hiring around 70,000 professionals each year outside the US (*Podcast 93*). Previously, she led British Army recruitment through a period of immense challenge and told me:

> *"Setbacks aren't roadblocks; they're the raw material for growth. Every challenge you overcome becomes a lesson you can use as fuel to drive your career forward."*

Your hardest moments can become your greatest assets - they will shape your resilience, sharpen your purpose, and empower your leadership in any storm.

Resilience Is Not a Solo Pursuit

Real resilience isn't forged in comfort or routine. It is shaped in the midst of adversity - when everything you value is on the line. **Colonel David Richmond**, now CEO of the Royal Hospital Chelsea (*Podcast 98*), lived through a moment that redefined his life and leadership. He told me:

> *"The most intense moment of my career happened during a Taliban ambush. As they opened fire, a bullet tore through the back of my right thigh and exited through the front. I was knocked unconscious. In the midst of chaos and injury, I learned the true meaning of resilience and teamwork as my comrades saved my life and supported me through a gruelling time. While the physical recovery was tough, the emotional part was the hardest."*

Enduring leaders lean into their teams, draw on collective strength, and emerge from adversity transformed.

The Courage to Be Vulnerable

Jon Macaskill, retired Navy SEAL Commander (*Podcast 278*), knows the cost of resilience. During *Operation Red Wings* in Afghanistan, portrayed in the film *Lone Survivor*, he was at HQ, responsible for real-time surveillance and radio communications. He listened as his friends' voices crackled over the radio - ambushed and outnumbered. Then came the moment every leader dreads. A rescue helicopter was shot down. Jon told me:

> *"The powerlessness I felt, knowing my friends were in mortal danger and I couldn't do anything, was crushing. I ended up with complex PTSD. It's the invisible wound of war, a constant reminder of the horrors we witnessed. It took a long time, and a lot of support, to even begin processing what happened that day."*

Resilience is not about never breaking, but how you respond in the aftermath. Accept help, confront pain, and rebuild. In business, your "ambush" may be an unexpected crisis or setback. Your response becomes the standard for your team. Lean on others, accept vulnerability, and do the work to heal and grow.

Resilience is learned, not inherited.

Be the Victor, Not the Victim

Some seasons bring relentless blows. I endured an *"annus horribilis"* - the unexpected bereavement of my brother David, the knife attack on my brother Graeme, business challenges, even a personal health crisis. Alone in a hospital bed, lost and uncertain, I reached a low point. My mother's words returned:

> *"Be the victor, not the victim."*

I fought back - seeking counsel, drawing on stoic philosophy, talking to my wife Leigh and focusing only on what I could control.

When crisis hits, ask yourself:

"What have I learnt, and what will I do now?"

Setbacks are inevitable. Your response makes the difference. The best leaders do not avoid hardship - they burn it as fuel for wisdom and compassion. I learned to seek wise counsel, invest in growth, and drop the mask of invulnerability. Deliberate action and honest vulnerability build your own resilience and your team's, too.

New Approaches

The skills that got you here will not always serve you in future storms. Growth often requires leaving behind habits, sharpening new skills, and seeking direct feedback - most powerfully through 360° reviews. The strongest leaders practise new techniques, share them, and surround themselves with advisers willing to speak difficult truths.

The Three Hums

At fifty-three, **Anthony Scaramucci** (*Podcast, 379*) had achieved the kind of boardroom success most leaders could only dream of. Yet nothing humbled him more than being *"smacked in the mouth and politically chain-sawed"* after just eleven days as the White House Communications Director for President Donald Trump's first term.

That was the toughest valley on his Life Map.

As every seasoned CEO and field commander knows, true leadership is not revealed in triumph but in how you rise after a spectacular fall.

Anthony's journey is a masterclass in humility. He owned his mistakes, rebuilt his reputation and refused to sacrifice integrity for ambition; even when the stakes were at their highest. Under the pressure of public failure and betrayal, he learned fast.

He turned defeat into wisdom, led with renewed empathy and chose principle over expediency.

Anyone can lead when everything is going well; when the wins come easy, sales are rising, profits are doubling. The real challenge comes when times get tough, when storms hit and headwinds blow, when you have to make painful decisions - and the pressure is real.

In every world-class organisation I have coached, the difference between teams who thrive and those that just survive comes down to three qualities - what I call: *The three Hums: Humility, Humanity and Humour.*

Humility is your compass; quiet confidence, open curiosity and the readiness to seek input rather than lead from ego.

Humanity is your anchor; genuine care for those you lead, the willingness to listen and the courage to connect at a human level.

Humour is your release valve, especially the self-deprecating kind. It keeps you grounded; helps you adapt and shows your team that even in the hardest moments there is room for perspective.

On the topic of humility, **The Right Honourable Sir Vince Cable** (*Podcast 381*), has a life dedicated to public service and global impact. From economist and diplomat to Cabinet Minister, academic, business leader, and celebrated author, he has shaped policy and inspired progress across continents, industries, and generations.

When I asked him, "How do you keep grounded, keep your humility and not get too full of yourself?", he told me:

> *"I don't know how much was just instinct and how much was sort of checking myself, not to get too self-important. I also used to travel around on public transport, even when I was Secretary of State, I didn't have a red box. I had a red plastic bag that I used to carry around on the trains. I still do use the buses, just chatting to local people, it keeps you grounded, as you say. I think it's very tempting to be opinionated and believe that you know better than everybody else. So, you have to challenge yourself constantly."*

Every leader, whether on the battlefield, in Parliament or in the boardroom, is called to stay humble, keep learning and face the hard times with integrity. That is how you build wisdom, and inspire trust that stands the test of time.

When it comes to humour, I am reminded of four leaders, veterans from the Special Forces, all of whom have faced a shared crisis on Everest: **Al Carns** (*Podcast 364*), **Anthony 'Staz' Stazicker CGC** (*Podcast 396*), **Garth Miller**: Pilot, Gurkha and SAS Major and **Kev Godlington**: renowned adventurer and entrepreneur (*Podcast 387*).

When an avalanche swept their team towards disaster, there was a moment of stunned silence. They checked on one another, then chose gratitude over fear. With a roar of laughter, they rallied and went on to summit Everest in world-record time.

When you lead with humility, humanity and humour, you set the tone for resilience and you inspire those around you to dig deeper, adapt faster and achieve more than they thought possible.

Control the Controllables

Adam Koch, a leader I coached as Global Retail Director of Travelex (*Podcast 334*), now CEO of Sweat in Australia, faces the daily reality of a degenerative eye disease that is slowly taking his sight. Adam told me:

> *"Losing my sight has forced me to focus on what I can control: my attitude, my response, and the way I lead my team through uncertainty. I can't change what's happening to my eyes, but I can choose to show up with courage and positivity every single day."*

Adversity is never a question of if, only when. When it strikes, focus on what you can control and let go of what you cannot. This is not about shutting down your emotions; it is about gaining greater emotional regulation and the inner strength to keep going. In every crisis, ask yourself:

"How much energy am I wasting on things beyond my influence?"

The world's top performers - whether CEOs, elite athletes or military leaders - channel their energy into action, not anxiety. They know the power of what **Mel Robbins** calls the *"Let Them Theory"*: you can't control what *others* do or say, but you can always control *your response.*

Devon Harris OLY (*Podcast 103*), Jamaican Defence Force officer, three-time Olympian and member of the legendary Cool Runnings bobsleigh team, is a masterclass in resilience. His journey from the streets of Kingston to the Olympic stage is a story of grit. Devon told me:

> *"The journey to achieving greatness isn't always about glory. It's about the sacrifices and setbacks that test your resolve. Even in the toughest times, like when I was delivering pizzas to make ends meet just before the Olympics, it's not about quitting on your vision, but adapting and pushing forward, no matter how tough the road ahead seems."*

That is the essence of Stoic leadership. Focus on what you *can* influence, accept what *you cannot* and keep moving.

Wing Commander Jacqui Wilkinson's journey (*Podcast 388*) is another testament to tenacity and the transformative power of choice. She's a gold medallist in the military heptathlon, a commanding force in the RAF and she's the author of *Turning the Tables on Trauma: A Survivor's Story of Child Sexual Abuse.*

Jacqui has faced many of life's deepest wounds. Yet her story is not defined by adversity. It's defined by the way she's risen above it. Speaking at the Inspiring Leadership Foundation's 'Ride to Inspire' charity cycle, she shared a message that resonates for every leader:

> *"Your past does not define you. It's how you rise from it. You don't choose your hand, but you do choose your legacy."*

Resilience isn't about dodging adversity; it is about transforming setbacks into opportunities to advance. **Chris Cecil-Wright** (*Podcast 221*), models this after a near-fatal hang-gliding accident. He transformed his life, leaving the Army to become a global yacht broker and explorer. Chris told me:

"Resilience is about adapting to change, bouncing back from setbacks and finding a way forward even when things get tough. I've learned to embrace new challenges, push beyond my comfort zone and never let fear hold me back. Whether it is climbing mountains or building a business, the greatest rewards come from facing our fears and proving our capabilities."

Resilience is about moving forward, embracing change, and staying unbowed.

LEADERSHIP WISDOM

General Sir Mike Jackson GCB CBE DSO (*Podcast 126*), former Chief of the General Staff, sadly died in 2024. A few months earlier I had corresponded with him. He was terminally ill with cancer, yet you would not have known it from his upbeat manner. Mike was a character; calm, collected and resolute, especially in moments of high stakes. His leadership was defined by resilience, moral clarity, and refusal to be cowed by pressure.

During the Kosovo conflict in 1999, as Commander of NATO's Kosovo Force, he clashed with U.S. General Wesley Clark over an order to seize Pristina airport - a move he deemed strategically unsound, and dangerously escalatory given the presence of Russian forces. When told to block the runway, Mike famously refused, telling Clark:

"I'm not going to start the Third World War for you."

His refusal stood, the situation was resolved diplomatically, and his ability to speak Russian smoothed a fraught moment. It was a masterclass in strategic judgement and moral courage - doing the right thing even when it was hard.

Mike said:

"Never let setbacks break you. In the face of adversity, stay calm, assess the situation and make the best decision you can with the information you have. It's about having the courage to do the right thing, even when it's difficult."

General Mike showed impressive reserves of resilience. It gave him the strength to face intense pressure and high stakes with composure and moral clarity, the true hallmarks of resilient leadership.

YOUR CALL TO ACTION

Turbulence will come. What will define your legacy are the habits, mindset and decisions you make in the storm.

- **Build resilience with disciplined action**. Choose one new habit and commit to it for 21 days.
- **Prioritise rest and recovery**. Model this for your team - your stamina sets the pace.
- **Run a pre-mortem**: ask what could go wrong in three years, then prepare today for those risks.
- **Reflect deeply on past setbacks** and the lessons you learnt - this becomes your crisis playbook.
- **Lead with vulnerability as strength**. Model openness in three ways this month.
- **Choose one developmental challenge** that stretches you and set a clear deadline.

The best leaders shape culture, build clarity and establish habits that help their teams emerge stronger after any storm. Simplicity, discipline and integrity are your anchor in turbulent times. Lead from the front, knowing that today's actions become the foundation for tomorrow.

YOUR NEXT MISSION

The **Resilience Quotient (RQ)** is more than a personal shield; it is the foundation of reputation. When you and your team adapt, recover, and learn from adversity, you earn trust and respect.

Turning to the **Brand Quotient (BQ)**, remember: your customers and your team are watching, especially when the pressure is on. **Cécile Frot-Coutaz**, CEO of Sky Studios (*Podcast 135*), whose leadership at Sky, YouTube and Fremantle was inspiring, told me:

"Authenticity is the foundation of great leadership."

It takes courage to live your values, discipline to keep your word and resilience to maintain your course. In every context, people follow those who set the example.

Your authenticity and resilience under pressure become the roots from which your culture, brand, and legacy grow. The leaders who are remembered are those who remain authentic, resilient, and unwavering in purpose.

*"You can't stop the waves,
but you can learn to surf."*

Jon Kabat-Zinn, *Wherever You Go, There You Are*

7
BQ – Brand Quotient:
Shape Your Personal Brand

What is BQ?

Your brand is not what you say about yourself. It's what others whisper about you
when you leave the room. As a leader, your
reputation is the silent compass that guides your
influence, your legacy and the loyalty of those who
choose to follow.

As **Stephen Covey** taught, your personal brand is built day by day,
through the *"emotional bank accounts"* you build up with colleagues, clients
and teams. Trust is your currency. Each act to build trust - a courageous
decision here, a candid interaction there - is a deposit that compounds
over time.

When trust is high, people follow not because they must, but because they
want to.

Assess Your Brand

The best leaders are perpetual students. They understand that mastery is
never final. They listen, adapt, and keep sharpening their skills until no one
can question their authority to lead. If you want to set the pace, step back
and assess your brand with brutal honesty. Where do you excel? Where do
you fall short? This is not about self-criticism; it is about self-mastery.

The answers cannot come from your own view. You cannot correct what
you do not know or what you refuse to see. The answers have to come from
those who witness you at your best and your worst.

As **Epictetus** said:

> *"It is impossible for a man to learn what he thinks he already knows."*

Once you know where you stand, act. Lean into your strengths. Address your gaps. Leadership is not a solo act; it is the legacy you leave etched in the hearts and minds of those you serve.

Gain Insight with 360° Feedback

One powerful lesson I share with CEOs and boards is to challenge their knowledge gaps. A useful tool for this is the *Johari Window*. It is a simple framework for building self-awareness and trust, showing the gap between what you know about yourself and what others see. Seek feedback, share openly, and expand your *"open area."* This promotes transparency and connection across teams, driving effective leadership. Openness and honesty form the foundation for genuine authority and trust.

Ask your team seven questions to learn how your brand appears to others - and how it can evolve:

1. What qualities in me do you admire and want me to keep?
2. What qualities could I add, in order to improve?
3. What behaviours should I stop?
4. What behaviours should I start?
5. What behaviours should I continue?
6. Where do you see me in five years?
7. How can I stretch myself to grow further?

This takes courage. It is an invitation to embrace discomfort, allowing truth to sharpen your edge.

Jamie Woods, Group CEO of JCW (*Podcast 252*), turned his business into a global recruitment powerhouse with relentless feedback and transparency at the core. Jamie told me:

> *"The 360° Feedback process is never easy. It is exposing and sometimes you hear things you would rather not. But if you're serious about growth, you have to lean into it. The real breakthroughs come when you are willing to listen, reflect and act on what you learn."*

Jamie's lesson: world-class leaders do not avoid feedback, they pursue it. Feedback is not just a tool; it is a discipline.

Et Halstead, CEO at JCW and recognised on SIA's *"40 Under 40"* list (*Podcast 273*), proved this, as he grew operations globally:

> *"360° Feedback is one of the most valuable tools for any leader serious about growth. It is not always comfortable but it uncovers blind spots and keeps you and your business moving forward."*

Dr Saul B. Helman, President of Epsilon Life Sciences (*Podcast 308*), embraced this discipline too. With humility and care, he put himself through the process alongside his senior team. Saul told me:

> *"The real power of the process is that it shines a light on the things my colleagues couldn't see themselves. It's not always comfortable but it's the only way to get a true picture of how you're showing up as a leader."*

The business case is clear. Over time, 360° feedback delivers a tangible return on investment, building self-awareness and accountability. More importantly, it anchors humility and resilience across leadership.

Stuart Haire, Group CEO of Skipton Group (*Podcast 246*), summed it up:

> *"The higher you climb, the easier it is to get insulated from real feedback. That's why I make it a priority to seek out truthful perspectives. It keeps me honest, helps me see my blind spots and reminds me that leadership is always a work in progress."*

World-class leaders keep studying themselves. Modelling a feedback culture at the top is also fundamental in helping every person in the culture grow.

Lead with Curiosity and Humility

Dan Helfrich, former Chair and CEO of Deloitte Consulting LLP USA (*Podcast 328*), built his leadership on curiosity, humility and service. Leading Deloitte through transformation, Dan shared with me:

"The most important lessons I've learned as a leader have come from listening, truly listening, to the people around me. When you approach every conversation with curiosity and humility, you create space for new ideas and build trust that fuels high performance."

Humility and the courage to be vulnerable, to ask questions and to keep learning - separates world-class leaders from the rest, especially in uncertain times. These qualities are key to understanding your brand and its potential. They drive high performance because teams feel heard, valued, and inspired to contribute. Their presence - or absence - can be heard in the whispers about you. When present, they spark deep loyalty and respect.

This was clear in my conversation with **Lieutenant General Tim Evans CB CBE DSO** (*Podcast 26*). Tim - Commander of the Allied Rapid Reaction Corps, Commandant of Sandhurst, SAS Troop Commander and SBS Squadron Commander - discussed the humility he'd seen in a leader he deeply admired:

"When I was ADC to General de la Billière - the most decorated general, a Special Forces leader, I respected that he was very humble. He could talk to the Queen, yet would be just as comfortable chatting with soldiers. He espoused 'mission command': delegate, but keep your finger on the pulse, and trust your people. As Field Marshal Slim said: leadership is being yourself."

In this conversation, Tim also reminded us that every person you meet has something to teach you about leadership, if only you are willing to listen. Let your actions speak louder than your intentions. Your brand is not built in one dramatic moment, but in the sum of consistent daily acts of integrity.

This point was reinforced by **Chris Barron**, General Manager at Unilever (*Podcast 276*). For decades, he led high-performing teams, putting people first and championing cultures where every voice counts. Chris told me:

> *"Leadership is about earning trust every single day; through your actions, your words and the respect you show to others. When you create an environment where people feel seen and heard, you unlock their best work and inspire loyalty that lasts."*

The true mark of a leader is not in the metrics left behind, but the character built within your team. The willingness of people to support each other, speak up, and go the extra mile because you have their back. That is how world-class results are delivered.

Let Your Story Be a Beacon

As you reflect on your journey, ask yourself:

"What are the moments that shaped me? How did I respond to adversity?
How can my story guide my next step and inspire those who walk beside me?"

Your story is the heartbeat of your leadership. It is much more than a list of wins and losses. Data persuades, but stories move people. They build the trust and resilience that numbers alone never can. When telling your story - in interviews, newsletters, or honest conversations with your team - speak with humility. Vulnerability is not weakness; it is the foundation of genuine leadership.

Keep your story true. Resist the urge to polish away every flaw. The most powerful stories include failures and fears too. That is how real connection forms and where real growth is born.

A Personal Story - Commit or Collude

Your brand is not built on what you say, but on what you do. One decision at a time. One test at a time. Each moment, you choose whether to commit or collude.

There are moments in leadership where exhaustion clouds judgment and mutiny stirs beneath the surface. I remember one such moment, high on a sun-scorched mountain track in Cyprus during the Double Mountain Marathon. Dust was thick in our throats, our boots ground against loose rock, and fatigue weighed heavily on every step. The summit was close, but spirits were frayed.

With me were two Scots Guards veterans of the Falklands War, Lance Sergeant Fleck and Piper Marshall - wiry, gritty, battle-hardened men. Piper Marshall finally broke the silence in his Scottish brogue:

"Hey, Lieutenant Perks, I cannae feel my legs. Let's have another rest, I can't go on..."

His words hung heavy - a challenge, not a plea. In that moment, I felt the pull to avoid conflict and let the team stop.

But real leadership is not about comfort. It is about making the hard call when every fibre in your own body craves relief. In business, as on that mountain, your brand is forged in those moments; when your team is close to breaking, when the easy path beckons, and all eyes turn to you.

Do you stop, or press on? Do you commit, or collude?

My father's voice echoed in my mind - sharp, uncompromising:

"Commit or collude."

You can collude with comfort, or you can commit, own the outcome, and carry the standard forward. I stared at both men, grabbed the front of their shirts and barked:

"We're running. Let's go."

We surged forward, shoulder to shoulder, stride after stride, and pushed up that mountain. We finished first on day one, and first again on day two, carving out a world record for what the Army still calls *"The Cyprus Walkabout."*

That single moment - the choice to commit - broke our deadlock and ignited our will. It taught me what I have since seen across military operations and boardrooms alike: courage and commitment are contagious. When one leader sets the standard, others rise to meet it.

Every CEO faces that moment. When pressure rises and fatigue sets in. When the team looks to you for relief. Do you collude with mediocrity, or do you commit to lead with courage, even when it comes at a cost? What standard will you choose to set?

Lieutenant General Robert Baxter CBE DSc FRSE FIET (*Podcast 38*), a distinguished British Army officer, offered a clear warning:

> *"Brand is all about consistency. Be clear about what you stand for and deliver on it, every time. Your reputation is built over time but can be destroyed in an instant. So be careful with the choices you make."*

That is the discipline of great leadership: to commit, with consistent action, especially when it matters most. That is what your people will remember.

Chart Your Own Course

My mother, Tricia, once dreamed of being an 'Admiral's Lady', quietly hoping after her husband's death that, as her son, I would carry that ambition for senior rank into reality. For a time, I imagined myself climbing to the very top of the British Army. But not all dreams should be inherited. Some you must forge for yourself.

Authentic brand-building sometimes means pausing to "smell the coffee" and ask yourself the hard questions. You have to trust your instincts, notice the subtle changes, and know when it is time to adjust your course. For me, that moment came with sobering, liberating clarity.

Out of 170 sharp and highly ambitious officers who entered the elite Army Staff College, only a handful would climb to the very top. I graduated in the top ten percent, but the truth was plain: the path to the highest ranks was narrow, the standards unforgiving and the competition relentless.

At crucial points in your career, take a step back and ask the questions that demand honesty and courage:

- *Am I truly suited to this organisation?* Does this environment bring out my best, or am I forcing myself into a mould that does not fit?

- *Do I have the knowledge, skills and attitude to excel?* Or are there gaps I must close?

- *Will I continue to grow here?* Is there a long-term career ahead, or have I plateaued?

- *Do I belong in this culture, among these values and these people?* Or am I hiding part of myself?

- *Is this how I want to spend the rest of my life?* Does the path ahead excite me and give me purpose, or is it time for something new?

These questions are tough, but they give you clarity and conviction when you face them honestly.

Embrace Change

After reflection, I realised I had to pivot - yet I waited. I hesitated, then delayed. It took a couple of years before I finally set a new direction. One lesson stands out:

Be firm in your decision and kind in your execution.

Comfort can be a trap. The most successful leaders move on when the time is right. If you are at a crossroads, consider reading *Who Moved My Cheese?* - a simple book, but full of wisdom on embracing change.

My own pivot began when I applied for one of the few fully funded places to take the Executive MBA, all while serving as 15 Brigade Chief of Staff. Many people advised against it, warning that it was not the obvious path for my career. Yet I had a longer-term plan. I lobbied to join the Army's Management Consulting Services and transformed that role into a springboard for my move into business - a journey that now includes founding my leadership firm and building the *Inspiring Leadership Podcast* community.

Jon Parry, a humble and accomplished leader (*Podcast 70*) spoke with me about his own experiences of pivoting. After twelve years as VP of Asda Logistics Services, where he built a reputation for operational excellence and leadership, he chose to move on, becoming Supply Chain Director at B&M Retail. Jon told me:

> *"Stepping away from a place where you have built your name isn't easy, but growth demands leaving your comfort zone. It's in those moments of uncertainty that you discover what you are truly capable of."*

His wisdom is clear. Leadership is not about holding onto past achievements. It is about facing forward, taking risks, and learning from every change. Trust your experience to guide you, even through the unknown. Jon believes every leader must commit to reflection and reinvention. That mindset not only unlocks your full potential, but it also inspires those who follow.

Empower Excellence

World-class leaders are measured not only by their own achievements, but by the legacy and reputation of the teams they nurture and inspire. Think about how you shape the brand of your team, fostering high performers whose reputation will grow over time.

Rohit Gupta, President and CEO of Enact Holdings USA, balances discipline with humanity at the executive level. He is known for building high-performing teams, and he uses a personal checklist not only for himself but for every leader in his care.

Rohit said:

"Leadership is about understanding your strengths and your element; making sure you and your team are playing to what you do best. It's not just about filling roles; it's about creating an environment where each person feels empowered to lead from their strengths."

Rohit's insight echoes **Sir Ken Robinson's** wisdom. Real excellence emerges when people are in their element, using their unique talents with passion. For Rohit, world-class leadership calls for designing teams where everyone is set up to thrive. When leaders match roles with strengths, they unlock potential for people and business alike. **Al Carns DSO OBE MC**, shares more on building thriving teams:

"Very carefully identify and select your team. Trust them - empower and delegate responsibility. Then release them, with very clear boundaries, to achieve those outputs and report back to you. Then go again, and keep going, until it becomes unstoppable."

Al balances freedom with clarity of direction and expectation, to empower excellence.

Sairah Ashman, Global CEO of Wolff Olins (*Podcast 240*), reminds us of the critical need for psychological safety and empathy:

"Lead with courage, fostering a climate where others feel safe to bring their whole selves to work and treat each person as they would like to be treated, not only how you would; that's how you create real impact."

Courage like this is not always loud. Often, it is steady. It encourages others to show up, take risks, and grow. The leaders who inspire are those who know themselves, lead from their values, and help others step up to be their best.

Duncan O'Rourke is CEO for Middle East, Africa and Asia Pacific at Accor (*Podcast 237*), and has over 30 years in hospitality, leading 130,000 people across 40 countries. Duncan told me:

> *"Inspiring leadership isn't something you can train for; it's something you grow into. It's about having a mission, a guiding principle and bringing people with you on the journey. When you empower your team, stay true to your values and celebrate diverse opinions, you create an environment where everyone can exceed their own expectations."*

Duncan reminds us that the leaders who inspire are those who know themselves, lead from their values, and help others step-up to be their best. Exceptional leaders are not defined by awards, but by the enduring success and reputation of their teams. When you invest in building a strong, authentic brand - for your team and yourself - you set a standard that inspires excellence long after you have moved on.

LEADERSHIP WISDOM

General Dame Sharon Nesmith DCB ADC Gen, Vice Chief of the Defence Staff (*Podcast 68*), is a beacon for building trust at the very top. Sharon's journey is a series of historic firsts. She became the first woman to command a brigade at division level and rose to be the highest-ranked female officer in British military history. When we spoke, her words were grounded in hard-earned experience:

> *"Building trust in leadership requires understanding and connecting with your team through personal relationships and authenticity, which is crucial in structured organisations like the Army. Inspiring leaders must adapt their style to each situation, focus on opportunities rather than barriers, use empowering language and continuously seek feedback to improve and foster a culture where everyone feels valued and respected."*

The best leaders blend strength with humility. They shape cultures where people are seen, heard and inspired to give their best. They adapt to the context, nurturing the team's brand as carefully as their own.

YOUR CALL TO ACTION

When a storm hits, your team will look to you - for clarity, calm, and conviction. These moments reveal true leadership. You and your team will either drift or steady the compass and set your course.

Here is how you can lead your people through turbulence and come out stronger:

- **Invite unfiltered truth**: Create opportunities for honest feedback from key stakeholders, ideally facilitated by someone independent and trusted. This isn't just a formality - it's about discovering how others genuinely experience your leadership. When done well, this process can reveal blind spots and help bridge the gap between your intent and impact.

- **Focus your fire**: From the feedback received, identify just two behaviours that would make the greatest difference in your leadership. Direct your discipline and energy towards these. They are your levers for meaningful change.

- **Show up and be accountable**: Thank every contributor for their honesty. Share with them two strengths you will double down on and two areas you will improve. Ask them to *catch you doing things right* in short feedback loops over the next year. This is more than accountability. It is visible proof of your commitment to grow.

- **Cascade the standard**: Extend this practice through your leadership team. Every leader deserves the same honesty. This builds not only individual growth, but a culture where transparency and trust are the norm. Anything less and ego, blind spots and drift creep in.

Lead in this way and you set a tone of courage, humility and relentless improvement.

YOUR NEXT MISSION

Your **Brand Quotient (BQ)** shapes the foundation of your professional reputation and the way others perceive your leadership. Your values and principles are the lens through which your reputation is judged.

Leadership grounded in integrity and responsibility shapes not just your brand, but the trust and respect of those you lead. This is the bridge to the next chapter - **Legacy Quotient (LQ)**. The true test of leadership is stewardship: lifting your people, strengthening your culture, securing your organisation's footing.

Legacy is the mark you leave behind after the titles are gone and the command has passed. It's not built in one triumph, or one crisis. It's built quietly, day by day, in the choices you make and the trust you nurture. So ask yourself:

"Will my leadership endure? Will my values ripple through generations of leaders and teams?"

In the end, a great CEO is measured not just by results while in the chair, but by whether the culture they've built stands strong, united, and innovative long after they have gone.

The next chapter will help you define - and build - that legacy.

8
LQ - Legacy Quotient:
Leave Your Enduring Leadership Imprint

What is LQ?

Your Legacy Quotient measures what endures when the titles are gone. Legacy is not a checklist of milestones or the sum of your trophies. It is the deep, lasting influence you have on people, organisations and communities along the way. Inspiring leaders leave a meaning-ful, sustainable mark that can withstand the years.

Whether you are leading a global enterprise or guiding a small team, your mission is constant: leave things better than you found them.

This is stewardship at the very heart of real leadership. Leadership is not a solo sprint; it is a relay race. Pass the baton with care, making sure those who come after are equipped to run faster.

A Personal Story - A Legacy of Service and Courage

My father, Lieutenant Commander Paul Perks, was a fighter pilot in the Royal Navy. He lived by a simple, but powerful motto:

"Don't die with the music still in you."

He led from the front, inspiring his fellow pilots and giving his all, right up to his last breath, losing his life after a catastrophic aircraft malfunction.

He was just 33 years old.

Years later, I read the letters his colleagues sent to our family. They revealed a leader who put developing others ahead of his own advancement. His legacy was unmistakable:

"Serve to lead."

During the Indonesian crisis, he commanded 801 Squadron, Fleet Air Arm, a fast-jet unit stationed in Singapore. Determined to keep his pilots safe, he personally tested every new aircraft. The Buccaneer jets were underpowered, plagued with defects, yet he refused to send his men into the unknown without knowing the risks himself.

On his last fatal flight, he was testing a newly delivered jet out of Changi. At full speed, a turbine blade snapped loose, severing the fuel lines and setting the aircraft ablaze. My father's voice, his co-pilot, Lieutenant Commander Bill White remembered, was calm and clear:

"We need to check this out. I'm bringing it in."

He ejected Bill, saving his life. Then, with the crippled aircraft, he fought for control until the very end.

Two days later, the news reached us in England. My mother, Tricia, opened the door to a smartly dressed Casualty Visiting Officer. In that instant, her world changed forever. Our family's story changed, too.

I share this with you because true leadership is not measured by the length of your command. It's measured by the impact you make, the lives you touch and the values you leave behind.

Years later, determined to understand the man I had never fully known, I reached out to my father's Royal Navy pilots across the globe and invited them to lunch at Sandhurst, eager to hear the stories that could fill the gaps in my understanding. One pilot, Roger, looked me in the eye and said gently:

"Jonathan, your father died in my jet - in my cockpit. By all rights, he should be here having lunch with you instead of me."

The room fell silent. Bill then leaned forwards and offered me a choice - a choice every leader faces at some point:

> *"You can be a victim, or you can be a leader. You can spend your life saying, 'Poor me', or you can make your father and mother your inspiration. Learn from their example. Stand on their shoulders. Take the lessons and build something that matters."*

That conversation helped me to take my father's example forwards: his legacy of service. I encourage you to consider the people who have inspired you. Which lessons are you taking forward as you shape your own legacy?

The Ripple Effect

One of the people I admire most is my wife, **Leigh Bowman-Perks** (*Podcasts 100, 300, 301 and 400*). Her determination is unwavering. She refuses to let other women and girls endure the pain she once faced.

In her book *Inspiring Women Leaders*, she opened a window into how adversity forged her strength and sense of purpose. Her journey, from humble beginnings to executive coach, speaker, podcaster, top team facilitator and, in 2016, Founder-CEO of the Inspiring Leadership Foundation, is proof that where you start in life does not dictate where you finish.

Leigh has dedicated herself to shaping leaders, cracking barriers for women and girls, and sparking practical, lasting change. Her vision is bold:

> *"Breaking down barriers and sparking a global movement for inspiring leadership, grounded in local communities, delivering real results."*

That clarity of purpose has already created ripple effects across the UK, Kenya and South Africa, changing lives one at a time.

Zara Lachlan (*Podcasts 331 and 361*) became the first female, and youngest person, aged 21, to row solo across the Atlantic from Europe to South America. She covered 4,366 miles, 97 days, unsupported and broke three world records. Zara told Leigh:

> *"I hope my solo Atlantic row will leave a legacy to inspire others, particularly women and girls lacking confidence, to overcome fear and chase their dreams. If it doesn't exist, make it exist. Do it. And somebody will follow your example."*

This is legacy in action - a story that empowers, magnifies courage and multiplies hope. As inspiring leaders, we must never underestimate the power of purposeful action, or the legacy we build when we invest in something greater than ourselves.

Take **Emma Kane**, CEO of SEC Newgate (*Podcast 118*), a powerhouse in global communications and leader of teams across five continents. Building and selling Redleaf Communications, championing major philanthropic causes, serving on boards that shape the future of health, culture and finance - Emma truly leads with intention. During our conversation, she shared how a crisis became a motivational driving force in her leadership:

> *"My 9-month-old son, Patrick, was rushed to the hospital having contracted meningococcal septicaemia. He was one of the sickest children who ever survived, nearly dying and losing his leg and fingers during a 4-month hospital stay. As I sat with him, I noticed vital equipment labelled 'COSMIC', Children of St Mary's Intensive Care. I realised that, despite being in a National Health hospital, this charity-funded equipment was keeping my son alive. That's when I knew I wanted to do more for charities."*

Often, the moments of deepest challenge can be the greatest influences on the legacy we wish to create. Leaders like Leigh, Zara and Emma remind us: leadership isn't just about what you achieve. It's about how you use your influence to create ripples of positive change.

The Starfish Story

Some days in your own leadership journey, the challenge will feel overwhelming. The odds stacked, the work like a drop in the ocean.

Picture a boy walking along a sun-scorched beach, strewn with thousands of stranded starfish. He picks one up, tosses it gently back into the sea. A passer-by laughs and calls out:

"Why bother? You can't save them all. Does it make any difference?"

Unfazed, the boy carefully picks up another starfish, returns it into the sea, and says:

"It made a difference to that one."

We can draw parallels with this well-known story when we think about creating a legacy. A legacy is not built through grand gestures alone. You cannot fix everything at once. What you can do is transform something. Small, consistent acts of care and courage, even if they touch just one person at a time, can create a remarkable and lasting impact.

Voices of Legacy

The most valuable resource you have is not money, but *time*. If you live to 80, you will have around 4,000 weeks. Guard them fiercely. Spend them well. Once spent, they cannot be reclaimed.

Dreams shift. Expectations collapse. Life rarely unfolds as imagined. In those moments, find meaning not in what was lost, but in what remains. There is wisdom, even in the ruins. Each day, I aim to pour everything into what I do, leaving nothing reserved, no potential untapped.
My motto reflects this:

"Live full - die empty."

What will echo after you are gone?

117

Lord Dr Michael Hastings (*Podcast 258*), who held major roles at the BBC, KPMG, and across philanthropy, told me that his legacy rests on one ambition:

> *"I hope it would say that I contended for the multitude. That I was an advocate for those without a voice. That I strove to make a difference. I gave everything I could, and those living on the margins, I gave them hope."*

He added, drawing on **Winston Churchill**:

> *"We make a living by what we get,*
> *but we make a life by what we give."*

His perspective is clear: build the world you want to see, instead of simply inhabiting the one you inherit.

Mike Amato (*Podcast 234*), having led across Washington Mutual and Barclays and written *The Better Way to Win*, told me his ambition was simple but profound:

> *"I want those I've worked with to say,*
> *'Mike helped me grow, helped me discover more of myself, and in doing so, I went far beyond what I thought possible'."*

Mike's ripple effect is evident in the many alumni he has helped shape, some becoming CEOs themselves. His legacy is not only results, but the generations of leaders he has raised. How you live today will shape the story that outlasts you. Take time to clarify the legacy that you want to leave to ensure your actions align.

Every Conversation Is a Chance to Learn

Legacy is not just what you passively leave behind. It is also what you pass on in the present through stories, insight and encouragement.

Over 400 guests on the *Inspiring Leadership Podcast* have reinforced this truth for me - that every conversation, if you listen, can shape you.

Simon Brewer (*Podcast 107*), host of *The Money Maze Podcast*, told me:

"The greatest opportunities in life come from the relationships you nurture and the questions you dare to ask. Every conversation is a chance to learn."

Simon's belief is simple. Networks thrive on curiosity, generosity and service. Genuine leaders listen first, ask deeper questions, seek to learn, and unlock doors for others. That is legacy in action: the gift of leaving every person, every encounter, every team stronger than you found them.

LEADERSHIP WISDOM

Consider **Field Marshal Lord David Richards GCB CBE DSO DL** (*Podcast 298*). Throughout his career, he led operations in East Timor and Afghanistan, commanded NATO forces, served as Chief of the General Staff (CGS) and, ultimately, became Chief of the Defence Staff (CDS), which is the professional head of Britain's armed forces.

In our conversation, we addressed a crux point in David's leadership: his command in Sierra Leone in 2000, where he defeated brutal rebels and protected many lives. His actions to avoid bloodshed required ingenuity and moral courage. He shared:

"In Sierra Leone, I knew I could do more than what I was ordered to do, but I couldn't openly disobey orders. I had to find a way to achieve my objectives while appearing to follow instructions."

Leaving a meaningful legacy can sometimes require finding thoughtful, principled ways to bend rules when necessary - not out of defiance, but out of a deep commitment to what must be accomplished.

YOUR CALL TO ACTION

A leader's role is not simply about ownership - it is about stewardship. A leader is entrusted to leave things better than they were.

- **Elevate your position**: Consider how you have improved your role since you stepped in. Identify three meaningful changes you will commit to, starting now.

- **Shape your legacy**: Think of three ways you can lift your people, so their achievements outlast your own time. True leadership prepares others to grow.

- **Close the gap**: If you were to leave today, what would people say? What do you hope they would say? The space between those answers is where your next effort lies.

Legacy is more than results. It is how you lift others, how you protect what matters most, and the stories you inspire in those who follow.

YOUR NEXT MISSION

Legacy does not appear only at the end. It starts in every decision, every challenge, every relationship you touch on your way. It connects your values, your sense of purpose, your resilience, your brand and your record of performance.

At the successful completion of my airborne selection and the parachute jump course, I was presented with my coveted parachute wings. The ceremony is a blunt 'pass' or 'fail'. From driving tests to climbing Everest, people appreciate the certainty of a binary result. Yet leaving a legacy is far more complex, with its many shades of grey. You can always try again, shaping your legacy through each decision. Two sayings have served me well. The Brazilian saying: *In the end, everything will be okay. If it's not okay, it's not yet the end.* Also, an Irish folk saying: *What's meant for you won't pass you by.*

The final duty of any inspiring leader is to leave the organisation, its people, and its culture in better shape than when they arrived. In the end, your legacy is not what you took for yourself, but how you inspired others to reach higher, dream bigger, and carry the flame forward. That is world-class leadership. It is within your grasp.

"Never doubt that a small group of thoughtful, committed citizens can change the world.
Indeed, it's the only thing that ever has."

Margaret Mead, Cultural Anthropologist

9
Navigate True North:
Master Your Integrated CEO's Compass

Integration:

Just as explorers trust their compass to guide them, CEOs must rely on their own integrated compass. During turbulent times, it is easy to drift and lose your bearings. That is when it is vital to pause, recalibrate, and set your True North once more.

The path ahead will test you. Yet, with the compass in hand, you can navigate uncertainty, inspire trust, and deliver results built to last. Bringing together the eight Principles of Inspiring Leadership - purpose, values, wellbeing, relationships, confidence, performance, reputation and legacy - gives you the focus and foundation needed to excel.

The world-class leaders I coach, who command boardrooms and inspire movements, share something in common. In the crucible of leadership, they earn respect not for the titles or credentials, but for their attitude. They combine daring ambition with discipline and the humility to listen deeply to those they lead. They work hard to build teams and causes greater than themselves. Their pursuit of learning is constant. **Laurence Everitt**, EVP Northern Trust (*Podcast 184*), captures it well:

> *"Every time I push myself to learn something new, I discover just how much more there is to master. Growth isn't a destination. It's a discipline, a habit you have to choose every day."*

His maxim is simple: never settle.

Leadership, like charting a course on unknown seas, is a continuous journey of growth, challenge and discovery. The CEO's Compass is not a static diagram, but a living guide to keep you true to your values, purpose and direction, even when the seas are rough.

The best leaders never stop recalibrating their compass. They pause, reflect and adjust course as threats or opportunities arise. That is not indecision - it is leadership maturity.

Navigate the 45° Line

If you have stood on a parade square before inspection, or at a boardroom table before a billion-pound deal, you know what that tension feels like. The greatest learning always sits just at the edge of fear. When you are living above The 45° Line - where your challenges stretch beyond your current abilities - that is when transformation becomes possible. This is where leaders are forged and where your story can become a beacon for others.

Living Above The 45°

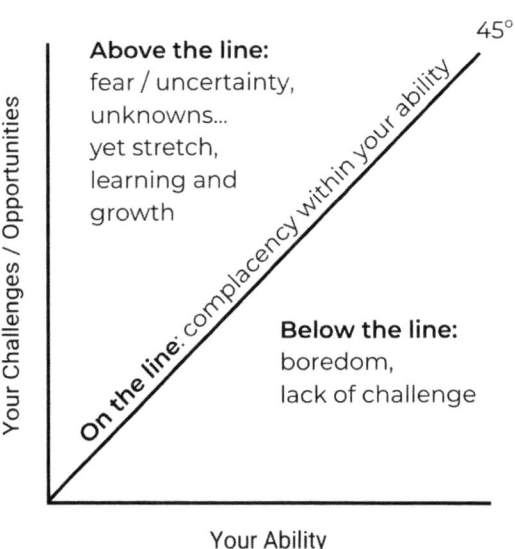

Picture this graph. Your comfort zone sits where the y-axis of challenge meets the x-axis of ability. Competence is built here, but true achievement lies beyond it.

The best leaders know the real magic happens above the line. Above the 45°, there is discomfort, there is risk, and failure is possible. Yet this is where growth lives.

When I coached a CEO through a transatlantic acquisition, she hesitated - uncertain about crossing into the danger zone. With clarity of mission, trusted advisors and relentless after-action reviews, she closed the deal and ignited her business. As **Admiral Bill McRaven** said:

> *"If you want to change the world, sometimes you have to slide down the obstacles headfirst."*

True leadership means choosing to live above the 45° line. Build teams that run toward challenges, not from them. Prepare for crisis, not comfort. Ask yourself:

"Where am I and my team on this graph? Are we stretching daily, or hiding in the comfort below the 45° line?"

Above the line is where the most is asked of you, and also where the most is given back.

Turn Failure Into Fuel

Joe Foster, Founder of Reebok and an unforgettable guest (*Podcast 145*), is proof that setbacks can become fuel. From humble beginnings to a global brand, his journey is a masterclass in resilience, risk and learning from every turn. His autobiography, *Shoemaker: The Untold Story of the British Family Firm that Became a Global Brand*, is uplifting. Joe told me:

> *"You don't learn from success, you learn from the setbacks, the mistakes and the times when things didn't go to plan. Every failure is a lesson in disguise, and it's those lessons that shape who you become as a leader and as a person."*

His wisdom runs deep. The true measure of leadership is not how you handle your victories, but how you respond to adversity. In our conversation, Joe spoke about staying curious, asking questions, and not allowing fear of failure to paralyse you. For Joe, greatness is not about avoiding mistakes. It is about using them as stepping stones. That mindset founded Reebok, and it is the same mindset that will keep you and your business moving forward when the winds turn against you.

Turn Difference Into Strength

Mastery is not given. It is earned through setbacks and honest reflection.

Dyslexia, for me, was once a limiting label. An early teacher called me *"stupid and thick"* - a voice that followed me for years. In time, I reframed it. Dyslexia became my superpower. It gives me a helicopter view. I can connect dots that others miss and see patterns in complexity. That skill became indispensable in boardroom crises, all formed from what some saw as a weakness.

Barnaby Davis, CIO for the Charities Aid Foundation, lives this approach. He told me:

> *"I have seen colleagues getting caught in the minutiae of an issue and being unable to operate and plan a way out and forward. I step back and see the whole landscape. It's about knowing when to zoom in or zoom out, when to focus in and always making sure actions align with the organisational objectives and strategy."*

What others call *disadvantage*, the best leaders turn into an edge.

Shift Perspective

In the thick of a crisis, perspective is the first casualty. Emotion narrows your sight. Tunnel vision takes over. This is why you need tools that widen perspective. **Marc Pettican**, EVP at Mastercard and former President of Barclaycard Payments (*Podcast 151*), was clear:

> *"Seeking honest feedback is crucial for growth as a leader. Don't be afraid to ask direct questions and encourage others to be candid with you, even if it's uncomfortable. It's the only way to identify blind spots and areas for improvement."*

Here's a practical method - *"Your Best-Friend's Perspective"*:

- Step 1: Ask yourself:
  "If my best friend faced this challenge, what advice would I give them?"
- Step 2: Write it down in one clear sentence.
- Step 3: Speak it out loud.
- Step 4: Act - now take your own advice.

The wisdom is within you. Usually, you already know the answer, you simply need space to see it. Another tool is *"The 10-10-10 Method"*. Ask:

"How important will this be in 10 weeks? 10 months? 10 years?"

Paul Fisher, SVP for Diebold Nixdorf Global Service Delivery, said it plainly:

"I wish I'd learned the value of slowing down and being more deliberate in my actions. It's not always about speed and efficiency. Sometimes, it's crucial to take a step back, reflect and truly understand the impact of our decisions, especially when they affect the lives and livelihoods of others."

Perspective clears the fog and brings wisdom, not panic.

Lessons from the Journey

"Too soon old, too late smart."

I've carried this proverb with me throughout my leadership. Growth comes, often, after speaking that hardest phrase:

"I was wrong."

My old IBM boss, **Ginni Rometty**, always reminded us:

"Growth and comfort don't coexist."

There is truth there - breakthroughs come only when you embrace discomfort, seek feedback, and let humility sharpen your judgment. **Rory Paterson**, Global Vice President at Expedia, is a leader I respect for his humility, openness and his knack for drawing the best out of global teams. He told me:

> *"Never be too proud to seek and accept advice, regardless of the source. Humility is vital in leadership."*

Listen Without Judgment

In my early career, I was quick to defend and slow to listen. I mistook vulnerability for weakness. Now, however, the most inspiring leaders I coach admit they don't have all the answers. They ask for help and listen genuinely. **Chris Pyle**, Headmaster of Lancaster Royal Grammar School and Chair of the Boarding School Alliance (*Podcast 182*), told me:

> *"Listen with the intent to understand. Don't just hear words, truly absorb what's being said. Consider perspectives and grasp their meaning. Listening transforms relationships and creates understanding."*

Air Vice-Marshal Bob Judson (*Podcast 283*), is another leader who exemplifies this well. After a distinguished career as a Jaguar pilot and senior leader, he transitioned to Deloitte and hosts an excellent podcast: *Leading 4 Life*. He stated:

> *"You have two ears and one mouth. Use them in that proportion. Leaders tend to talk more than they listen. Take the time to truly hear what your team says. They often have valuable advice and insights to offer."*

Real influence is rooted in listening. That is when trust grows, perspectives shift and cultures change.

Ronel Lehmann, CEO of Finito Education (*Podcast 137*), reinforced the point:

> *"True leadership is about making space for others. Listening without judgment. Supporting without expectation. Openness and empathy create the trust and safety that allow people to thrive."*

For Ronel, leadership is about building bridges, not walls. That is legacy.

Pay It Forward

The deepest satisfaction does not come from what you achieve alone - it comes from lifting others as you climb. This is not just sentiment. It is a leadership principle.

The story of young **Trevor McKinney**, from the film *Pay It Forward*, captures it well. For a school project, he set out to create a chain reaction of kindness. His idea was simple. Perform three good deeds for others, and ask them not to repay you, but to help three more strangers in return. One act sparking another, and another, until it grew into a movement.

The most inspiring leaders I coach multiply their influence by serving others, sharing knowledge, opening doors and empowering new leaders. At Sandhurst, we lived by this motto, as my father had:

> *"Serve to Lead"*.

That mindset lies at the heart of the Integrated CEO's Compass. Leadership is service. Service becomes legacy. By paying it forward, you create ripples that transform teams, shape culture, and move whole organisations. Not for recognition. Not for immediate reward, but to leave your mark on the future.

To build a culture of resilience and generosity, start with one act: mentor, share a hard-won lesson, open a door for growth. These small actions, much like **Admiral McRaven's** advice to make your bed each day, set the tone for all that follows.

I call it TNT: Tiny Noticeable Things. Small, but with explosive power. In the end, your legacy is not measured by the scope of your title or the span of your tenure. It is found in moments of service; acts of generosity and the people you elevate. That is the mark of a leader who inspires.

Mentorship, listening and vulnerability are strengths. Revealing your struggles shows others it is safe to be honest about theirs. These habits strengthen organisations, forge future leaders and create lasting bonds.

The Inner Compass

Every leader carries an inner section to their compass. The outer ring is shaped by the eight Principles of Inspiring Leadership. Yet at the centre lies something deeper - your energy, your commitment, and your willingness to put these principles into action.

Your compass revolves around four key areas: my self, my relationships, my organisation, and my society. Think of each as a unique lens, offering a fresh perspective on how the eight principles guide your leadership every day. Ask yourself:

"How much energy am I truly investing in each of these areas? Where am I thriving, and where am I neglecting what matters most?"

1. My Self

Leadership always starts with you. Before you can hope to inspire others, you must lead yourself - with honesty, discipline and courage. The truth is simple yet unrelenting: the decisions you make and the actions you take ripple outward.

I had the privilege of coaching **Professor Sharon Peacock CBE FMedSci**, a renowned British microbiologist and Master of Churchill College, Cambridge (*Podcast 191*). She is celebrated for her pioneering work in pathogen genomics, especially her leadership of the COVID-19 Genomics UK Consortium. Sharon told me:

> *"Self-belief is crucial. It's that inner conviction that you can do it, even when faced with challenges, setbacks and doubts. Trust in your abilities and embrace your ambitions fully. Spend less time doubting yourself, doubting your potential and more time moving forward with unwavering confidence."*

Hari Budha Magar MBE, a double-amputee and Everest mountaineer (*Podcast 291*), told me this as he reflected on his climb:

> *"Looking back, I wish I'd understood the importance of self-belief. Don't be afraid to dream big and pursue your passions, even if they seem daunting. With determination and perseverance, you can achieve remarkable things."*

Leadership begins with inner conviction. If you do not believe in yourself, you cannot expect others to believe in you.

2. My Relationships

Great leadership is shaped by the quality of your relationships - at work and at home. The energy you invest in the people who matter most sets the tone for your team, every single day.

Expiring leaders, unlike inspiring leaders, surround themselves with yes-men. They operate inside a bubble and depend on fear and control, rather than trust and transparency. In my work coaching CEOs and executive teams, I've seen this pattern repeated: leaders who only want good news, who avoid tough conversations, who close their eyes to problems.

Building authentic, trusting relationships is how you hold yourself to account.

Richard Bourne, CEO of Martins Properties (Podcast 76), knows the importance of escaping insularity and echo chambers. He returned to the theme of listening:

> *"One of the most valuable lessons I learned is to listen more than you speak, especially as a leader. It's tempting to dominate conversations, but by truly listening to your team, you'll gain valuable insights and perspectives that can inform better decisions."*

Listening builds trust. Trust builds unity. Unity drives performance, and sustained performance, over time, creates enduring legacies.

3. My Organisation

Every organisation's culture is shaped in the quiet moments. The decisions you make when no one is watching, the standard of discipline you either enforce or allow and as a leader, your behaviour is your organisation's mirror.

Curt Hess, U.S. Executive President of Vitesse and former CEO of Barclays U.S. Consumer Bank, reminded me how vital perspective is. In leadership, seeing beyond your own vantage point can make all the difference:

> *"Never underestimate the value of empathy and being able to see things through your opponent's eyes."*

Empathy is not softness. It is clarity.

Steven Fine, CEO of Peel Hunt (*Podcast 367*), has set a powerful example of how to drive culture and performance in tandem. Under his leadership, Peel Hunt is known for its collaborative spirit, unwavering client focus and dedication to nurturing talent at every level. Steven told me:

> *"You and your executive team set the tone. When you invest in culture with intention and courage, you don't just drive results. You build an organisation people are proud to belong to, and a legacy that endures."*

The standards you choose will outlast you. That is the hallmark of responsible leadership.

4. My Society

Leadership does not stop at the edge of the office car park. Real leaders extend their influence outward into the communities and societies they serve. **Patrick Kane**, Disability Ambassador, author, TEDx speaker and businessman (*Podcast 131*), summed it up:

> *"Looking back, I wish I'd realised sooner how important it is to give back to the community, no matter your situation or status. Helping others, disabled or not, to achieve their goals is possible, if you are willing to step up."*

Chris Barton, Founder of Shazam and visionary tech entrepreneur (*Podcast 363*), brought this idea alive in the world of innovation. He told me:

> *"What else could I come up with that people could do with it? If I could come up with a new idea, wow, just thinking of the opportunity, all these people walking around with this device in their pocket, and all they can do is make phone calls and send text messages. So those three things all coming together led to the idea for Shazam."*

When you create something new for your community, you can deliver lasting value to society. Looking for ways to give back - through service, invention or opportunity - shapes a better world for everyone. My friend of many years, **Major General Himalaya Thapa** (*Podcast 366*), once led major UN Peacekeeping Operations and directed rescue missions after the Nepalese earthquakes. He spoke with a true soldier's conviction:

> *"As leaders, we have to be an example to others and keep society safe. To be there when your people and your community need you."*

Leadership is never for you alone. It is for the society that counts on you.

A Lasting Compass

Your journey as a leader is never finished. Stay true to your values. Keep learning. Never lose sight of your True North.

In doing so, you will build not just an organisation, but a legacy. This will not happen all at once. It will happen in the way all great journeys do - one decision, one relationship, one day at a time.

LEADERSHIP WISDOM

Some of the best leadership lessons I've ever learned didn't come from a boardroom, but from the side of a mountain.

As a young Army officer with the Scots Guards, I found myself leading a team in the Cyprus Double Mountain Marathon - a gruelling global competition famed for testing the limits of endurance and strategy. We trained hard for three months but what set us apart wasn't just our fitness - it was our deliberate planning and preparation.

The maps were years out of date. Every day, we scouted the terrain, marking new tracks, roads and villages that no one else saw because they weren't on the map. We refused to rely solely on what we had been handed. Instead, we made the ground our own - studying every inch, updating our plans, owning the challenge.

On race day, our edge showed. We knew the landscape better than anyone else.

Leadership in business is no different. Hard work gets you to the starting line, but it is preparation, adaptability, and taking ownership of your path that makes the difference. You win by seeking what others overlook, and by adjusting your course when the ground changes below your feet.

After two years of relentless training and competition, our efforts paid off. Five of my teams finished in the top ten - and my own three-man team set a new world record.

T.S. Eliot once wrote:

"We shall not cease from exploration, and the end of all our exploring will be to arrive where we started and know the place for the first time."

Leadership is a journey of continual discovery. The edge is earned through relentless curiosity, purposeful preparation and the courage to make the map your own. In the Cyprus Double Mountain Marathon, I learned a lesson every leader should remember:

Maps change, but a good compass never fails you.

YOUR CALL TO ACTION

As you complete this compass journey, treat these final steps as your own operations briefing:

- **Score yourself honestly**: mark each compass element out of 100. Inspect what you expect.
- **Check your quadrants**: for self, relationships, organisation and society - ask where you invest energy, and where you neglect it.
- **Amplify strengths**: lean into what you do best.
- **Close gaps**: name the weaknesses that hold you back, and take steps to improve.

Your leadership is not defined by perfection, but by courage, accountability and relentless forward action.

Your Legacy Starts Now

Life does not hand out guarantees.

I remember sitting in the cardiologist's office, hearing words that could have been a full stop. An ending. But I chose to see them as a comma. A pause, followed by possibility. That was not the day my story ended. It was the day my story changed direction.

In that moment, I made a promise. I would not merely survive. I would not simply outlast the odds. I would outlive them, and I would out-lead them. I would live, not just longer, but better. I would live with intention, every single day.

None of us knows how many pages are left in our storybook. Each morning places a fresh, blank page in front of us. What we write on that page will never be erased. Each choice, each word, each act of courage becomes part of our legacy.

Not some day in the future. Not on the final page. But *today*. This is the gift we have been given.

My hope is that somewhere in these pages, through the voices of the leaders I have coached, through the wisdom of those I have served beside, and through the lessons of those I've interviewed and learned from, a seed has been planted for you. A spark has been lit. A challenge has been issued. To rise above the title on your business card, beyond the corner office, or the organisational chart. To be remembered not for the position you held, but for the *difference you made*.

That is my legacy.

But the real question is this: what will yours be?

This is your moment. These are your pages. Do not just read these words. Live them. The world is not waiting for perfect leaders. It is searching for courageous ones. People willing to look in the mirror with honesty, to own their story without excuse, to grow when it's easier to stand still, and to raise the standard of leadership for those who walk behind.

You *already* carry the tools. You already hold the insight. With them comes responsibility.

Epictetus, the Stoic philosopher, put it this way:

"We don't choose our hardships, but we do get to choose how we respond to them."

That is leadership. Not the rank, not the medal, not the office - but the response.

So, take command of your compass. Set your course. Go where others need you most. I am reminded of my mother's words, a Quaker line that has guided me through battlefields and boardrooms:

"I shall pass this way but once. Any good that I can do, or any kindness I can show to any human being, let me do it now. Let me not defer nor neglect it, for I shall not pass this way again."

Legacy is not built in grand moments. It grows, quietly, in one act, one choice, one day at a time. In how you treat those who cannot repay you. In discipline over distraction, service over self, resilience over resignation.

The truth is that your legacy is already being written.
Every decision is ink on that page. Every day, another line.

You do not need to wait.

Permission is not required.

Your legacy starts now.

Go. Live it. Lead it.

Inspire leadership.

Warm regards
Jonathan

Jonathan Bowman-Perks MBE

"Life is a journey, not a destination. The end of one chapter is simply the start of another."

Inspired by the writings of Ralph Waldo Emerson

10

Inspiring Leadership Podcasts

I t is my pleasure to include a list of the first 400 *Inspiring Leadership* podcast episodes.

You will recognise the names of some of these distinguished guests as they have influenced the creation of this book. I hope I have whetted your appetite to find more wisdom in their stories.

Visit https://jonathanperks.com/podcasts/ for links to the podcasts hosted on YouTube, Apple and Spotify.

Podcast Episode	Name	Role
1	Lieutenant General Sir Nick Pope KCB CBE	Deputy Chief of the General Staff, Master-General of the Ordnance, Command in Afghanistan and Bosnia
2	Dame Alison Nimmo	CEO - The Crown Estate
3	Major General Paul Nanson CBE	Commandant - The Royal Military Academy Sandhurst
4	Professor Philippa Snare	SVP - The Trade Desk (Meta & Microsoft)
5	Colonel Jorge Mendonca DSO	CEO - Gascoigne Estates
6	Anna Hemmings OLY MBE	Britain's most successful female kayaker
7	Alistair Kett	Partner - PwC, Adjutant 1 RRF
8	Brigadier James Richardson MBE	CEO - Haig Housing Trust
9	Colonel Tim Collins OBE	CO - Royal Irish, SAS Officer, Author
10	Air Marshal Sir Graham Stacey KCB CB QCVS MBE RAF	Commander of British Forces Cyprus

11	Jonathan Bowman-Perks	Month 1 review of Podcast Insights
12	Richard Fenning	Global CEO - Control Risks
13	Nathan Newton-Willington	Personal Trainer: Fitness & Nutrition
14	Colonel Jonny Gray	Senior MD - Ankura, specialising in sport
15	Paul Cleal	Former Partner & Board Member - PwC
16	Ashok Gupta	Chairman & CEO of multiple businesses
17	Alexander Knigge	SVP - Corporate Comms, Marketing & Brand (Digital) - Emirates Group
18	Jonathan Bowman-Perks	Month 2 Review of Podcast Insights
19	Alison Hutchinson CBE	CEO - Pennies Digital Money Box charity
20	James Knight MC	Royal Marines Officer & Financial Advisor
21	Fiona Lambert	Award-winning brand creator & MD - Harpenne
22	Colonel Garry Hearn	Divisional Director - UK Defence Academy
23	David Heron	Group CEO - Wilton & Bain
24	Colonel Tim Wilson OBE	CEO - MSI Global Alliance, Ex QDG
25	Roger Steare	Corporate Philosopher, Advisor on Ethics
26	Lieutenant General Tim Evans CB CBE DSO	Commander Allied Rapid Reaction Corps, SAS, SBS officer
27	Jonathan Bowman-Perks	Month 3 review of Podcast insights
28	Alderman Sir Peter Estlin	The Lord Mayor of London
29	Catherine Baird	SVP - Emirates Cabin Crew Training
30	Colonel Chris Wakerley	KPMG Partner, business owner, Army CO
31	Nousheh Paris	VP - American Express
32	Lieutenant General Sir James Bashall CB CBE	Parachute Regiment, Commander Home Command and Strategic Advisor
33	Mike Still	Chair YPO Scotland & NED roles

34	Sir William Russell	The Lord Mayor of London
35	Stefan Barden	CEO & NED - Growth & Turnaround
36	Jonathan Bowman-Perks	Month 4 review of Podcast Insights
37	Annette Barnes	CEO - Lloyds Banking Group, Private Bank
38	Lieutenant General Robert Baxter CBE DSc FRSE FIET	Deputy Chief of Defence Staff (Health)
39	Fiona Hathorn	CEO Women on Boards, diversity champion
40	Mark Pollack	MD - Aston Chase
41	Nick Borwell	Associate Fellow of Said Business School, Oxford
42	Alex Chisnall	My Podcast Mentor - *Screw It Just DO It* Podcaster
43	Matt Oppenheimer	CEO - Remitly Global, Seattle USA
44	Sherilyn Shackell	CEO - The Marketing Academy
45	Major General Alastair Dickinson CBE	VP - KBR, RE Commando and Director General of Army Basing
46	Peter Holiday	COO - LAMDA, Mountaineer
47	Peter Kavanagh	Chairman - Leaders Romans Group
48	Caroline Goyder	*Gravitas* author, voice coach, speaker
49	Martin Williams	CEO - Gaucho and M restaurants
50	*Episode withheld*	*To maintain guest confidentiality*
51	Major General Chip Chapman	Paratrooper, Strategist, Counterterrorism
52	Renier Lemmens	CEO, Chairman - fintech and payments
53	Major General Jonathan Shaw CB CBE	Chairman, Army Commander, SAS, Cyber Pioneer
54	Danny Payne CMG	CEO - Foreign & Commonwealth Office Services, Global Infrastructure Leader
55	Andreas Utermann	CEO - Allianz Global Investors

56	Major General Paul Nanson CB CBE	Commandant - The Royal Military Academy Sandhurst, Leadership advisor
57	Barry Leahey MBE	MD - Advisor, Exports, Global Growth
58	John Cresswell	CEO - Bibby Line Group, Ex CEO of ITV
59	Tracey Groves	CEO - Intelligent Finance
60	Jonathan Bowman-Perks	Insights on leadership in crisis
61	Lieutenant General Sir James Bashall CB CBE	Parachute Regiment, Commander Home Command and Strategic Advisor
62	James Batchelor MBE	CEO - Alertacall: *"I am okay"* button
63	Mark Hodgkinson	CEO - *SCOPE* charity, Virgin Money
64	David Ringwood	Psychologist, Assessment & Coaching
65	Lieutenant General Sir Nick Pope KCB CBE	Deputy Chief of the General Staff, Master-General of the Ordnance, Command in Afghanistan and Bosnia
66	Oliver Johnson	*Reflections From a Deep Pool* Podcast
67	Joe Copeman	Global SVP - ACAST for Podcasts
68	General Dame Sharon Nesmith DCB ADC Gen	Vice-Chief of the Defence Staff, First female Army General, Moderniser
69	Martin Dougherty	COO - Wellcome Sanger Institute
70	Jon Parry	VP - Asda Logistics Services, now B&M
71	Brigadier Jim Richardson MBE	CEO - Haig Housing Trust, Bosnia, Iraq
72	Christopher Leek	World-record ultra-endurance athlete
73	Colonel Garry Hearn OBE	Divisional Director of Defence Academy
74	Derek Kehoe	CEO - BNP Paribas, Ireland country head
75	Angie Klein	CEO - Visible, SVP Verizon, Growth Leader
76	Richard Bourne	CEO - Martins Properties
77	Sir William Russell	692nd Lord Mayor of London, finance leader, pandemic

78	Major General James Cowan CB DSO	CEO - HALO Trust charity, Landmine Clearance Leader, Afghanistan, Iraq.
79	*Episode withheld*	*To maintain guest confidentiality*
80	Deanna Oppenheimer	CEO - Barclays Retail, Chairman & NED - IHG Hotels Chair, Thomson Reuters, Slalom
81	Alistair Kett	Partner - PwC, Adjutant 1 RRF
82	*Episode withheld*	*To maintain guest confidentiality*
83	Richard Fenning	Global CEO - Control Risks
84	Oliver Johnston	Founder - Stepping Out from the Top Team; Coach and Mentor to Jonathan
85	Chuka Umunna	MP - Shadow Business Secretary, Board Advisor, ESG Banking
86	Kate Oliver	Motorcycle Tour Leader - Himalaya Expeds
87	Izzy Fox	VC - Luminous Ventures, Deeptech Investor
88	Dr Ruth Wandhofer	NED - Fintech leader, author, PhD
89	Colonel James Cameron CBE	VP - Leadership Initiatives for Walmart
90	Leila Woodington	Marketing Director - Meta, North Europe
91	Colonel Lucy Giles	President of Army Officer Selection Board
92	Mike Hope-Milne	Enterprise Director - Pearl & Dean
93	Cath Possamai	Talent Acquisition Director - Amazon
94	General Sir Rupert Smith KCB DSO & Bar OBE QGM	DSACEUR NATO, Commander 1st (UK) Armoured Division in Gulf War, GOC Northern Ireland, Author
95	Nick Hine	Employment Lawyer - Constantine
96	Guy Waites	Skipper - Solo / Round World Yacht Race
97	Josh Graff	MD - Linkedin, EMEA & LATAM
98	Colonel David Richmond CBE	CEO - The Royal Hospital Chelsea
99	Paul Cooper	Leader - M&A advisor to growth companies

100	Leigh Bowman-Perks	CEO - Inspiring Leadership Foundation
101	Professor Philippa Snare	SVP - The Trade Desk (Meta & Microsoft)
102	Professor Angus Laing	Executive Dean - Heriot-Watt University
103	Devon Harris OLY	JDF Officer - Jamaican Bobsleigh Team, 3-time Olympian as in film *Cool Runnings*
104	Anita Liu Harvey	Director - Spotify, Global Payments
105	Anna Baird	Chief Customer Officer - Gen AI GTM, Google, Global AI evangelist
106	Paul Bean	CEO - Bellrock Group, now advisor
107	Simon Brewer	CEO - Money Maze Podcast
108	Kevin Roberts	CEO - Red Rose, ex-CEO - Saatchi & Saatchi
109	Dr Todd Dewett	LinkedIn influencer, Best-selling speaker
110	Daron Seukeran	Group Medical Director of SK:N laser clinics
111	David Hartshorn	Skipper - Round the World Clipper Race
112	Will Hogg	MD - Kinetic Consulting, Ex-Army, ex-HRD
113	David Buxton	CEO of Arachnys, Regtech Founder
114	General Sir Richard Shirreff KCB CB	DSACEUR NATO, GOC 3rd (UK) Division, Commander 7th (UK) Armoured Brigade & Commanding Officer of the King's Royal Hussars
115	Charlotte Valeur	Chair of Institute of Directors (IoD)
116	Jim Brigden	CEO - Digital Marketeer, Led 4 x Exits
117	Scott Parazynzki MD	CEO - Fluidity Tech, NASA Astronaut
118	Emma Kane	CEO - SEC Newgate Comms & Chair roles
119	Andy Taylor	VP - Schneider Electric

120	Captain David Marquet	Captain - USS Santa Fe, *Turn the Ship Around!* and *Leadership Is Language* author
121	Derek Redmond OLY	World & European 4x400m champion, iconic Olympic finisher
122	Stan Phelps	*Goldfish* author, CX/loyalty expert, CSP
123	Danny Williams OLY	Judo 2014 Commonwealth gold, Olympian
124	Paz Avalos	General Manager - Sodexo, Operations
125	Jonathan Bowman-Perks	CEOs Trusted Leadership Advisor
126	General Sir Mike Jackson GCB CBE DSO	Chief of The General Staff, author and TV personality, Kosovo standoff, reformer
127	Dayna Steel	CEO - The Rock Business
128	Sandy Loder	Extreme Adventure Guide, Coach & Leader
129	Dr Marta Ra PhD	CEO - Paracelsus Recovery
130	Bo Brabo	From Battlefield - White House HR Chief - Boardroom - Podcaster
131	Patrick Kane	Young TED speaker, disability ambassador
132	Pamela Hackett	CEO - Proudfoot
133	Joel Blake OBE	Founder - GFA Exchange - Fintech StartUp
134	Nicole Ryan	Founder - Alex's Adventure
135	Cécile Frot-Coutaz	CEO - Sky Studios, ex-YouTube EMEA Head
136	Mikkel Iverson	Founder - Under One Sky, Social Impact
137	Ronel Lehmann	CEO - Finito, Mentoring Young People
138	Jeff Nischwitz	Life Changing Leadership Facilitation Coach
139	Michael Jacobsen	Producer - *Dirty Dancing*, Entrepreneur
140	Steve Foster	CEO - One Golden Nugget
141	Dr Margaret Casely-Hayford	Chair, Chancellor and NED

142	Brian Ashton MBE	Head Coach - England Rugby
143	Ann Pickering	Chief HR Officer, O2 (Telefónica UK), DEI
144	Roman Roberts	Ex-Army Interrogator, *RealTalk* Podcaster
145	Joe Foster	Co-Founder - Reebok
146	Dom Burch	Asda Social Lead, Retail Innovator, Coach
147	Brian Heyworth	CEO - Lansdowne Partners
148	Jonathan Bowman-Perks	Review of 147 Podcasts – leadership lessons
149	Richard Thorpe	Ex-London Irish rugby, Canada World Cup
150	Graham Harle	Global CEO - Gleeds
151	Marc Pettican	President - Barclays Payments now Executive VP Mastercard
152	Walt Rakowich	CEO - Prologis, *Transfluence* author
153	Larry English	President - Centric Consulting
154	CEO Podcast #1	CEOs discuss - Brand, Reputation & Trust
155	Paul Howarth	CEO - National Nuclear Laboratories (NNL)
156	Steven Kuhn	*Unleash Your Humble Alpha* author
157	Sir Peter Wanless CB	CEO - NSPCC, President Somerset Cricket
158	Paul Denman	Partner Close Brothers Asset Management
159	CEOs Club Podcast #2	CEOs discuss - Lessons from the Pandemic
160	Julie Baker	VP - Hilton Hotels, London Luxury & Ireland
161	Seamus Smith	CEO - JDX Consultants, ex-Sage Pay CEO
162	Barbara Cox-Lovsey	Nutrition Entrepreneur, Nutrichef & Author

163	CEOs Inspiring Leadership Forum #3	CEOs discuss - Strategy technology and digitisation
164	Liz Baitson BEM	Director - High Net Connect, Philanthropy
165	Mark Fleiner	President Malvern Panalytical Instruments
166	Huw Owen	CEO - Ark Data Centres, Royal Hong Kong Police
167	Lane Belone	Green Beret, *Unleash Your Humble Alpha* author
168	Graeme Newell	Behavioural Finance & Brain Science
169	CEOs Inspiring Leadership Forum #4	CEOs discuss - Leaving a legacy in your lifetime
170	Chris Moon MBE	Landmine Survivor, Champion of Resilience
171	Ahmed Khan	CEO - Neurosurgical Biotechnology
172	Darren Moorcroft	CEO - Woodland Trust
173	Emilio Antonio Guevara	CEO - Free Enterprise & Capitalism
174	Brian J. Esposito	CEO - Esposito Intellectual Enterprises
175	Gary C. Laney	CEO - Success Masters LLC
176	CEOs Inspiring Leadership Forum	CEOs discuss: best tips you were given
177	Sophie Neary	MD - Retail Consumer Google UK, ex-Meta
178	Rodney C. Flowers	Defied paralysis: walked beyond prognosis
179	Manly Hopkinson	Skippered world's toughest yacht race
180	George Wight	Managing General Partner - Legacy Exchange, Family Office PE, Dealmaker
181	Major General Andrew Mackay CBE	CEO - Complexas, Helmand Task Force Commander, led Musa Qala assault
182	Chris Pyle	Head - Lancaster Royal Grammar School
183	Belinda Agnew	MD - Enamus, B2B tech digital branding,

184	Marty Martinez	US Army Command Sgt Major, Podcaster
185	CEOs club - Leadership	6 CEOs discuss leadership
186	David Harney	President - Great-West Lifeco, Europe
187	Guy Hands	CEO - Dealmaker: PE Triumphs & Trials
188	Stephynie Malik	CEO - SMALIK Enterprises, Crisis expert
189	Kwame Kwei Armah	Artistic Director - The Young Vic Theatre
190	John Hewett	Founder - Jackson Hewitt and Liberty Tax
191	Sharon Peacock CBE	Master - Churchill College, Cambridge
192	James Felts	Ranger, 82nd Airborne, Helping Veterans
193	Brian Williamson	Entrepreneurship, Growth, Exits, Boards
194	Mark Leppard MBE	Headmaster - British School Abu Dhabi
195	Barry Habib	CEO - Market Forecasts, Shaping Housing
196	Michael Dean	Funding Innovation in Property Lending
197	Amandeep Kaur	CEO - BLACKDOT, Redefining Community
198	Richard Browning	CEO - Gravity, Jet Suit Human Flight
199	Prashant Gami	CEO - Innovation, Scaling, Tech for Good
200	General The Lord Dannatt GCB CBE MC DL	House of Lords, Head of the British Army 2006-2009
201	Yilmaz Erceyes	Chief Marketing Officer Premier Foods
202	Daniel Bernard	CEO - Investment, Innovation, Sports Data
203	Melanie Richards CBE	NED - Championing Board DEI
204	Nando Cesarone	President - UPS, From Loader to Leader

205	Martin Wilson	CEO - Digital Identity Net, Creating OneID
206	Leendert Den Hollander	VP - GM Nth Europe, Coca Cola Partners
207	Bob Gappa	CEO - Growing Brands: Franchise Strategy
208	Dan Ziegler	Entrepreneur, Polymath, Tech Coy Founder
209	Graham Brown	Building Brands Through Global Storytelling
210	Josh Hug	Co-Founder, COO - Remitly Global
211	Seumas Kerr CBE	MD - The D Group, ex-Major General
212	Roger Weatherby	Chairman - Weatherbys Banking Group
213	Corina Burton	From Adversity to Leadership Unstoppable
214	Carrie Hilton	Disrupting Construction Industry Media PR
215	Sarah Mukherjee MBE	CEO - Driving Diversity in Sustainability
216	Episode 1: The Inspiring Leadership Podcast partners	Graham Brown & Jonathan Share Insights
217	The Hon Dan Jarvis MBE MP	Cabinet Minister, *Long Way Home* author
218	Bruce Lyman	CEO - Board Wisdom & Military Leadership
219	Garrett Kinsman	Decentralising Internet, Connecting Billions
220	Episode 2: MQ	Graham Brown & Jonathan Share Insights
221	Chris Cecil-Wright	Super Yacht broker, Daring Explorer
222	Steven Kuhn	Review of Jonathan's Peruvian Retreat
223	Robert Vass	Shaping Europe's Global Security Future
224	Harry Matovu KC	Barrister & King's Counsel, Brick Court

225	Episode 3: PQ	Graham Brown & Jonathan share insights
226	Rene Yoakum	Remitly - Growth Through People Power
227	Lieutenant General Sir Simon Vincent Mayall KBE CB	*Soldier in the Sand* author. War, peace, Middle East insights
228	Lameen Abdul-Malik	Nobel Prize award winner
229	Episode 4: HQ Part 1	Graham Brown & Jonathan Share Insights
230	Craig Mahoney	CEO - University Vice-Chancellor
231	Ankur Sinah	Chief Product Technology Officer - Remitly
232	Marjet Andriesse	Transforming Tech Leadership Across Asia
233	Episode 5: HQ Part 2	Graham Brown & Jonathan Share Insights
234	Mike Amato	Turning Crisis into Culture Change
235	Grant Baldwin	CEO - Speaker Lab and Author
236	Saema Somalya Kaukab	EVP - Navigating Risk, Scaling Trust Globally
237	Duncan O'Rourke	CEO - Accor Northern Europe
238	Episode 6: CQ	Graham Brown & Jonathan Share Insights
239	Mustafa Bartin	Changing Retail, Blending Online - Offline
240	Sairah Ashman	Global CEO - Woolf Olins, Building Iconic Brands with Purpose
241	Major General David Rutherford-Jones CB	CEO - Morden College charity & former Commandant at RMAS
242	Episode 7: EQ	Graham Brown & Jonathan Share Insights
243	Colonel Roland Ladley MBE	*Sam Green* MI5 series author
244	Rachid 'Ben' Bengougam	SVP - Human Resources EMEA at Hilton
245	Episode 8: RQ	Graham Brown & Jonathan Share Insights

246	Stuart Haire	Group CEO - Skipton Building Society
247	General David H. Petraeus	Partner- KKR, Former Head of CIA
248	Sam Instone	CEO - AES International, Life Guards Officer
249	Amliya Antonetti	CEO - Designing Genius, Human Behaviour
250	Darrin Jahnel	CEO - Jahnel Group, Scaling Culture
251	Episode 9: BQ	Graham Brown & Jonathan Share Insights
252	Jamie Woods	Group CEO - JCW Group, Exec Search
253	Sarah Woolnough	CEO - The King's Fund, Asthma & Lung
254	Craig Hatch	President - Tetra Tech, Europe & UK
255	Episode 10: LQ	Graham Brown & Jonathan Share Insights
256	Jordan Berman	Creative Storytelling Wins Brand Attention
257	Christian Scotland-Williamson	Barrister and 2-sport professional athlete
258	Lord Dr Michael Hastings of Scarisbrick CBE	Championing Inclusion, Impact, Global Good, Black Business Advocacy
259	Steven Cooper CBE	CEO - Aldermore Bank Group
260	Colonel Jim Hutton OBE	Colonel RM, Capt Australian Navy, Coach
261	David Sole OBE	School for CEOs Edinburgh
262	Inspiring Leadership review	Graham Brown & Jonathan Share Insights
263	Andrew Griffiths	Naval Officer, Leadership Strategy Coach
264	Brian J. Esposito	CEO - Founder, Investor and advisor
265	Dame Sara Thornton DBE QPM	UK Independent Anti-Slavery Commissioner, Chair of the National Police Chiefs' Council
266	Dr Karuna Ramanathan	Ex Singapore Naval Captain turns Coach

267	Serena Gordon	MD - Hoffman UK, Transforming Lives
268	Jamie Waller	Dyslexia, grit, building unsexy empires
269	Michael Welch OBE	CEO - Changing Industry & Online Impact
270	Admiral Mike Manazir	Captain USS Nimitz, Top Gun pilot, Author
271	James Sommerville	VP - Global Design at Coca Cola
272	Kevin Hogarth	CPO - KPMG/ Freshfields /Capital One/EY
273	Et Halstead	CEO - JCW Group, Executive Search
274	Craig Valentine	World Champion Speaker & Speaker Coach
275	Douglas Field	CEO - East of England Co-op
276	Chris Barron	GM - Personal Care UK & Ireland Unilever
277	Mark Aston	SF Soldier, *SAS Sea King Down* author
278	Jon Macaskill	Navy SEAL Commander to Mindfulness
279	Oscar Trimboli	*How to Listen* & *Deep Listening* author
280	Tim Creswick	CEO of Vorboss, London Fibre Network
281	Colonel Stuart Tootal DSO OBE	*Danger Close* author, Ex Colonel 3 PARA
282	Rob Metcalfe	Ex Royal Marine officer, leadership coach
283	Air Vice-Marshal Bob Judson	RAF Commander, Jaguar pilot, Ex Deloitte
284	Andy Wood OBE DL	CEO - Adnams, Deputy Lord Lieutenant
285	Dr Alice Maynard CBE	Champion Inclusion, Govern for Good
286	Robin Horsfall	SAS Soldier B Squadron - Iranian Embassy Siege
287	Colonel Andy Milburn	US Marines, *When the Tempest Gathers* author

288	Major Nick Garland	From battlefield trauma to tech
289	Commodore Peter Scott	Royal Australian Navy, Commander Subs
290	Justin Galliford	CEO - Norse Group, Unifying Culture
291	Hari Budha Magar	Everest Summit - Disabled Gurkha Hero
292	Herbert Lang	Harlem Globe Trotter, Kindness is Free
293	Justin Levene	Wheelchair Racer, Jiu-Jitsu Champion
294	Horst Schulze	Ritz Hotel & *Excellence Wins* author
295	Sareh Ameri & Faisal Al Nuaimi	7 Days 7 Emirates bike ride
296	Jessica Smith OAM OLY	Australian Paralympian Swimmer
297	Marc Allera	CEO - Consumer Division, BT Group
298	Field Marshal Lord David Richards GCB CBE DSO DL	Former Chief of the Defence Staff, Strategic leader in Libya, Afghanistan, Sierra Leone
299	Stephen M.R. Covey	*Trust and Inspire* co-author
300	Leigh & Jonathan Bowman-Perks	Review 300 guests Part 1
301	Leigh & Jonathan Bowman-Perks	Review 300 guests Part 2
302	Leah Tedrow	Strategic Marketing, Ride for Unity, UAE
303	Daniel Bernard	Entrepreneur and founder of Ride for Unity
304	Todd Gustafson	President of HP Federal LLC
305	Gavin Patterson	CEO, Chairman, Advisor, BT & Salesforce
306	Chip Massey	Ex-FBI Hostage Negotiator Special Agent
307	Pat Parsons	Mountain Rescue, RM Mountain Leader
308	Saul B. Helman MD	President - Epsilon Life Sciences
309	Jim Murphy	U.S. F15 Fighter Pilot
310	David Kasperson	*Trust and Inspire* co-author

311	Dr Stephen Barden	Strategic Partner, COO and CEO
312	Roland Rudd	Shaping Reputation, Powering Influence
313	Jimi Ibrahim	Lebanese view, 7 Days 7 Emirates bike ride
314	Justin Levene	Lessons learnt 7 Days 7 Emirates bike ride
315	Commodore Mike Deeks	Group MD Blue Ocean Marine Tech System
316	Jason Zintac	CEO - 6sense, Tech Entrepreneur
317	Vijay Tella	CEO - AI-powered Workato, Automation
318	Sarah Bolt	CEO - Forth, Health Tech & Biomarkers
319	Mandy Hickson	TEDx Speaker, RAF fast-jet Tornado pilot
320	Yosi Amram	Clinical Psychologist, spiritual intelligence
321	David Roberts	CEO - Verra Mobility, Smarter and Safer
322	Martin Gonzalez and Josh Yellin	Google Leaders, *The Bonfire Moment* authors
323	Philip Grindell	Former Scotland Yard Detective
324	Oz Alashe	CEO - Cybsafe, Special Forces Officer
325	Juan Jaysingh	CEO - Zingtree, Automate Customer Svc
326	Neil Basu QPM	*Turmoil* author, Metropolitan Police
327	Paul Biddiss	Military Advisor, TV movies script writer
328	Dan Helfrich	CEO - Deloitte Consulting LLP in the USA
329	Liran Belenzon	CEO - BenchSci, Decode Drug Discovery
330	John Browett	Chair - Octopus Group and IoD
331	Zara Lachlan	Solo Atlantic rower, 3 x World Records

332	Jeff Nischwitz	Life Changing Leadership Facilitation Coach
333	Heather Moyse OLY	2-time Olympian Gold Medallist
334	Adam Koch	CEO - Sweat, Female Fitness App
335	Major General Lamont Kirkland CBE	CEO - Team Forces. Founded £14M+ charity for military sport & adventure
336	Anthony Casa	President and CEO – Umortgage
337	Steve L. Blue	CEO - Miller Ingenuity
338	Archie Norman	Chairman - M&S plc
339	Rich Diviney	Founder - The Attributes, U.S. Navy SEAL
340	Admiral Bill McRaven	4-star Admiral, Navy SEAL & U.S. Special Forces Commander
341	Jonny Huntington	Disabled polar explorer and athlete
342	Jamie Waller	Entrepreneur, *The Dyslexic Edge* author
343	Colonel Kim 'KC' Campbell, MBA	Speaker, Author, US A-10 fighter pilot
344	Jon White	Kayaking world medallist, triple amputee
345	Pavita Cooper	Board Advisor, Chair of the 30% Club UK
346	Lynette Jackson	Chief Comms Officer - Siemens AG
347	Sam Mercer	CEO - Plantforce Rentals
348	Lieutenant General Sir Simon Vincent Mayall KBE CB	*The House of War* author. War, peace, Middle East insights
349	Rob Roy	CEO - U.S. Navy Master Chief Navy SEAL
350	Lisa Anne Bodell	CEO - Innovation, Simplification & Change
351	Admiral Sir Nick Hine KCB	CEO - Babcock Marine ex 2nd Sea Lord
352	Elizabeth Winfield	Secretary General - British Biathlon Union
353	Jason Fox	TV personality, former Royal Marine & SBS
354	Craig Cecilio	Start-up CEO and serial entrepreneur

355	Jilly Carrell	Beyond the Wire charity
356	Rob Israch	President - Tipalti, Scaling Fintech
357	Lieutenant General Sir Tom Copinger-Symes KCB CBE	Deputy Commander, UK Strategic Command, Rewiring Future Defence
358	Sally Orange MBE	Adventurer, Mental Health Campaigner
359	Captain Bill Wilson	Co-founder - Alchemy, U.S. Navy SEAL
360	Nandu Govindankutty	Senior Exec Roles, Product Champion
361	Zara Lachlan	Solo Atlantic rower, 3 x World Records
362	Liz McConaghy	Surviving, *Chinook Crew 'Chick'* author
363	Chris Barton	Founder of Shazam, Tech Inventor
364	Al Carns DSO OBE MC MP	UK Minister for Veterans and People
365	Jonny Huntington	World Record Holding Polar Explorer
366	Major General Himalaya Thapa	Nepalese Army Commander
367	Steven Fine	CEO - Peel Hunt Investment Bank
368	Matt Gallagher	Pro Rugby Player, Motor Neurone Disease
369	Prof Sir Cary Cooper CBE	Prof Organisational Psychology & Health
370	Mark Urban	Broadcaster, Journalist, Podcaster, Author
371	Will Casselton	CEO - McKinney Rogers
372	Dr Ferri Abolhassan	Board Member Deutsche Telekom AG & CEO - T-Systems International GmbH
373	John Peters	RAF Tornado Pilot in the Gulf War
374	Chris Duncan	MD - The Times & Media CEO, Board Director, CEO of Seedelta
375	Captain Emma Henderson MBE	EasyJet Captain, *Grounded* author
376	Scotty Mills	Royal Marine Commando, *Never Give In!* author
377	Sam Smith	CEO - SuperScalers, *The Secret Sauce* author

378	Zsuzsanna Recsey	CEO - Standing on Giants
379	Anthony Scaramucci	Financier, Entrepreneur, Powerhouse Voice
380	Chris Piehota	*Wanted: The FBI I Once Knew* author
381	The Rt Hon Sir Vince Cable	Politician, *Eclipsing the West* author
382	Damian McKinney	CEO - DioniLife, former Royal Marine
383	Colonel Simon Hutchinson	CEO - The Goldsmiths' Company, Regimental Colonel of the Royal Signals
384	Vishal Dalal	CEO - Pismo, Cloud Banking & Payments
385	Franklyn A. Butler	President & Group CEO - Cable Bahamas
386	Elke Anderl	CCO - T-Systems International
387	Kev Godlington	Mission Everest, SAS Soldier
388	Wing Commander Jacqui Wilkinson	*Turning the Tables on Trauma* author
389	Brian J. Esposito	CEO - Serial Entrepreneur
390	Neil Basu QPM	*Turmoil* author, Metropolitan Police
391	Kathleen Lucente	CEO – Red Fan Communications
392	Brigadier James Stevenson MBE	MD - Dscvry AI, Deloitte, Deputy Commander in Kuwait
393	Tobias Gutteridge	Founder – Bravery, *Never Will I Die* author
394	Air Commodore Rich Davies CBE	Jet Leadership, Innovating Air Power
395	Chris Silcock	MD - Kellanova UK & Ireland
396	Anthony 'Staz' Stazicker CGC	Founder - ThruDark, *The Hard Road Will Take You Home* author
397	Kate Griggs	CEO – Made by Dyslexia
398	Sir Stuart Atha KCB CB DSO	Director - BAE Systems, Deputy Commander RAF
399	Nabeel Kaukab	CEO - Jaan Health (Phamily) AI Virtual Care
400	Leigh & Jonathan Bowman-Perks	THE BIG ONE: Review 400 episodes

Endorsements

"Having led through war, loss, and public service, I know true leadership is tested in life's stormiest moments. The CEO's Compass is a vital guide for any leader - reminding us that clarity, compassion, and doing what's right matter most when the path ahead is hardest."

The Hon Dan Jarvis MBE MP - served with distinction as a Major in the Parachute Regiment, leading British troops on multiple operational tours and earning an MBE for courage and leadership. Following his military career, he has continued to serve with integrity as Minister for Security, Labour MP and Mayor of South Yorkshire.

"Inspiring, thought-provoking and filled with powerful life lessons, The CEO's Compass is the book we all need right now! In times of change, the one thing that should stay constant is your North Star. Jonathan Bowman-Perks shows you how to remain true to yourself and be successful in life and business. Read this book!"

Admiral William H. McRaven - retired four-star Admiral, former Commander of U.S. Special Operations Command. His legendary achievements include masterminding the raid that led to the death of Osama bin Laden. He commanded the capture of Saddam Hussein and led countless high-stake missions as Head of the U.S. Special Operations Command.

"Every successful leader needs a guiding star and the belief that the path towards that star is worth treading. What you believe determines how you think, who you are and what is important in life. Jonathan Bowman-Perks challenges us all to think again and perhaps reset our course."

General The Lord Dannatt GCB CBE MC DL - distinguished former Chief of the General Staff, leading the British Army from 2006 to 2009 after a remarkable forty-year military career. Now an independent member of the House of Lords, he is recognised for his outspoken advocacy for soldiers' welfare, his role in pivotal military operations in Northern Ireland, the Balkans, and Afghanistan, and his enduring influence as a respected voice on leadership and national defence.

"In the world of global finance and dynamic markets, navigating turbulence with clarity is crucial. 'The CEO's Compass' provides actionable strategies gleaned from extraordinary leaders, offering a vital guide for any executive striving to inspire and drive results whilst doing it with humility."

Anthony Scaramucci - bold financier, entrepreneur, and powerhouse voice who famously served as White House Communications Director for President Donald Trump, before becoming one of his most outspoken critics.

"This is the handbook for leaders who refuse to drift - practical, honest, and forged in real-world adversity. If you want your team to thrive through chaos, start here."

"True leadership isn't about being unbreakable - it's about adapting, rebuilding, and leading with purpose. The CEO's Compass shows you how to do just that, no matter what comes your way."

Jason Fox - fearless adventurer, bestselling author, TV personality from "SAS Who Dares Wins", former Royal Marine Commando & Special Forces Operator, inspiring others by turning adversity into strength.

"The CEO's Compass is a masterclass in providing clarity - a cornerstone for empowerment. Jonathan Bowman-Perks shows how empowering teams starts with a clear True North because without clarity of purpose, giving control leads nowhere."

Captain David Marquet - US Navy captain and bestselling author who transformed leadership by empowering every team member to think, speak up, and act as a leader; revolutionising organisations by *"Turn the Ship Around"* and *"Leadership is Language"*.

"The CEO's Compass is a masterful guide for any leader navigating the uncharted waters of today's world. Drawing on lessons I've learned from decades confronting crisis, prejudice, and complexity on the front lines, I know the value of true compass points: purpose, courage, and humanity at the helm. Every CEO who reads this will find not just strategies for success, but a much-needed recalibration of what it means to lead with heart, conviction, and resilience in the toughest times."

Anil Kanti (Neil) Basu - distinguished leader and former Assistant Commissioner of the Metropolitan Police Service, renowned for being the highest-ranking British police officer of Asian heritage and the national head of Counter Terrorism Policing. Over a 30-year career, he championed diversity, spearheaded the response to major terrorist incidents, and became a powerful advocate for reform, accountability, and social justice within UK policing.

"True North. Before you can orient your compass and lead your team effectively, it is IMPERATIVE that you find true north in your personal life. Jonathan helps you orient your compass and move the needle in this MAGNIFICENT book. He shows the reader how to attack life with conviction, curiosity, and caring through deep personal experience assisted by a STUNNING array of "been there, done that" friends. You'll make a mess of your copy with dog ears, notes in the margins, and scribbled "do I really do that?" questions. Find a quiet time, take out your pencil and attack!"

Admiral Mike Manazir - a decorated U.S. Navy admiral, former Captain of the aircraft carrier USS Nimitz, and a Top Gun fighter pilot whose leadership credentials span from the cockpit to the Pentagon. As the acclaimed author of *Learn How to Lead to Win*, he is celebrated for his dynamic approach to inspiring teams, championing courageous leadership, and guiding organisations through turbulence with clarity and conviction.

"Being a good leader isn't something you can just talk up; it's something you have to do. To get things done, you need relationships that are based on actions, not words. This book sets out the actions you can take - learning from leaders across business, sport and the military - to set your leadership compass right, whatever's thrown your way"

Roland Rudd - visionary leader and trusted advisor, founder and Chair of FGS Global, renowned for guiding boards and CEOs through pivotal moments with focus, effectiveness, and passion for purpose.

"Jonathan's Book, The CEO's Compass: How to Navigate Your Team through Turbulent Times, is an essential guide for leaders steering through storms. With humility, clarity, and actionable insight, this book empowers you to steer your team with confidence and resilience. It's a powerful guide to turning chaos into opportunity and leading with purpose when it matters most."

Major General Himalaya Thapa - a 36-year career in the Nepali Army saw him rise to key leadership roles at home and abroad, including command positions, United Nations peacekeeping missions, and diplomatic appointments. Highly decorated and a graduate of Sandhurst, he is renowned for his strategic acumen, global experience, and lasting contributions to Nepal's defence and international standing.

"The CEO's Compass is a masterclass in purpose-driven leadership; practical, heartfelt, and unflinchingly honest."

"This isn't just a leadership book, it's a field guide for navigating the hard stuff with integrity, clarity, and courage."

"This book is vintage Jonathan: direct, insightful, and deeply human. He's helped shape how I lead, and now he's made that accessible to leaders everywhere."

Matt Oppenheimer - pioneering fintech CEO of Remitly Global, transforming lives globally by making digital financial services more accessible, secure, and trusted.

"This is not only a brilliant book but an important and timely one. The CEO's Compass elegantly combines the best advice from Jonathan's unique network of leaders with his own experience and perspectives. I learned plenty of useful tips from every page of this beautifully curated book and will keep on referring to it. It complements Jonathan's fabulous podcast series where many of these leaders are brought to life so well."

Brian Heyworth - CEO and Managing Partner of Lansdowne Partners, one of Europe's most prominent asset management firms. With a career spanning over 35 years across global financial markets, Brian is recognised for his strategic leadership and deep experience, having previously held senior roles at HSBC, Bank of America, and J. P. Morgan.

"In The CEO's Compass, Jonathan Bowman-Perks shines the light of leadership into the darkness of our times in organisations, teams, communities, nations, families and relationships. As he highlights, psychological safety is no longer a nice to have in organisations; the evidence is compelling that building and nurturing cultures of psychological safety is THE key factor in business and teams. The CEO's Compass is a call to action for leaders - a call to presence, a call to empathy, a call to vulnerability, a call for safety, a call for humanity. The stakes have never been higher in leadership, and Jonathan offers us the secret sauce for more influence and greater impact as leaders light the way through the darkness to our collective true north."

Jeff Nischwitz - Leadership Sherpa, Speaker and Transformation Coach, Think Again Leadership and true friend to Jonathan.

Acknowledgments

To my wife, **Leigh** - no words can truly capture my gratitude for your love, patience and unwavering belief in me. Through late nights and early mornings, through doubts, rewrites and setbacks, you have stood by my side with encouragement, kindness and laughter that always lifted me when I needed it most. This book, and the CEO's Compass you co-created, exists because of your steady presence and your rare gift for seeing the best in me, even when I lost sight of it myself. Leigh, my partner in every sense, your spirit fills these pages; this book is as much yours as it is mine.

To my family, you have been the compass points of my life. My daughters, **Harriet** and **Bryony**, have given me constant love, support and challenge. I am so proud of the remarkable women you have become and everything you have achieved. In **Sandeep** and **Mark**, you have chosen strong husbands and together you have brought two beautiful daughters, **Lyra** and **Sofia**, into our lives. I treasure every moment spent with my stepson **Daniel** - a fine Police Officer, husband to the bubbly **Kirsty**, and father to **Grace** and **Riley**. I cherish the dry and witty banter with my stepdaughter, **Alanadh** and her husband, **Liam**. Each of you fills my life with warmth, joy and perspective.

To my brother **Graeme**, you have been my wise surrogate father since I was two years old. You have walked beside me through every high and every low, offering love, wisdom and steady counsel. The quote from our old St Peter's school wall that you shared, *"A diamond is a lump of coal that stuck at it,"* has guided me many times, reminding me that perseverance is the foundation of strength.

To three of the most inspiring leaders that I had the privilege to learn from as my Commanding Officers at crucial stages of my life: **Major General John Stokoe CB CBE**, at 14 (Electronic Warfare) Signals Regiment in Germany, **Brigadier John Griffin**, SAS, at 2nd Division Signals Regiment and **General The Lord Dannatt GCB CBE MC DL** at The Green Howards.

Finally, I am truly grateful to the team who helped this book take shape. I would recommend the brilliant book coach, **Michael Heppell**, to any fellow author; his wisdom, experience and steady guidance made this journey not only possible, but purposeful. To **Christine Beech**, whose sharp editorial eye refined my words; to **Harriet Soni**, my daughter, whose English skills and editing over the last crucial month majorly enhanced this book; to **David Sloly** for his editing and storytelling wisdom; and to **Matt Bird**, whose artistry in typesetting brought them to life on the printed page - my heartfelt thanks.

I am deeply grateful to all the leaders who shared their wisdom - on the podcasts, in our coaching sessions, in top team offsite events, and throughout countless conversations. Their insights have shaped the heart of this book and made these lessons possible.

To my family, my mentors and my creative partners - thank you for helping me bring this story into the world.

About the Author

Jonathan Bowman-Perks MBE is your guide for transformational leadership at the highest level. With two decades as a British Army officer and 25 years in global business - including senior roles at PwC, IBM, and as a PLC Managing Director - Jonathan knows what it means to lead under pressure, build resilient teams, and deliver results when it matters most.

Recognised by Her Majesty Queen Elizabeth II with an MBE for his work training UN leaders who helped prevent the East Timor massacre, Jonathan brings operational discipline and deep humanity to the boardroom. He's coached over 1,500 senior leaders worldwide, and through his acclaimed *Inspiring Leadership Podcast* has interviewed 400+ world-class CEOs, Olympians, Entrepreneurs, Public Figures and Special Forces operators - sharing hard-won wisdom and tools shaped by real experience, not just theory.

Inside these pages, you'll gain practical strategies and candid insights that help you lead with clarity, courage, and character - even in the most turbulent times. It provides a new set of tools, thought-provoking parables, personal stories and insights from my guests with practical lessons. Whether a Senior Executive or CEO, Jonathan's mission is to empower you to chart your own course to a meaningful legacy, inspire exceptional performance, and navigate your team through whatever lies ahead.

Jonathan's Other Books

These books sit alongside *The CEO's Compass*. Each one gives practical help you can use right away. Many readers keep them close. They are short. Direct. Easy to share with your team.

You can read them on your own for quick ideas you can act on today. You can discuss a chapter at a time with your leadership team. You can use the prompts in coaching and off-sites.

You can find them on Amazon or on <u>jonathanperks.com</u>.

Inspiring Leadership

This is a straight-talking guide to leading with values and clarity. It blends real stories with simple tools. It asks you to set your standards and live them. It helps you bring people with you when pressure rises.

Inside, you will find clear checklists for hard decisions. You will find questions that sharpen your thinking. You will find habits that build trust over time.

This book helps CEOs and founders who want a steady hand. It helps new leaders who want a firm start. It helps teams that need a shared language and focus.

These leadership lessons, drawn from Jonathan's own life and from the remarkable leaders he has worked with, are designed to help you navigate transitions and overcome business leadership challenges.

Each insight is built on hard-won experience in the military and the boardroom, offering tools you can apply in your own leadership journey.

Top Tips for Inspiring Women Leaders

This compact book shares lived experience from women who lead. It is practical and direct. You can open any page and find a tip you can use today. The ideas help you raise your voice, claim your space, and support others to do the same.

Inside, you will find bite-sized tips from leaders across every business sector and industry. You will find confidence builders you can practice in minutes, along with calm, effective ways to navigate bias and pressure. There are also tools for sponsors, allies and mentors.

This book helps women at every stage of leadership, from emerging talent to seasoned executive. It empowers them to find and use their voice, speak with confidence and claim their space at the table.

The tips and wisdom inside help allies who want to support with skill and respect, and teams that are ready to welcome more voices and diverse perspectives.

It contains an extra section on 'Top Tips for Effective Meetings'. Other leaders find these practical tips invaluable and we believe you will do so too.

This book is best used by picking one practical tip each day and reflecting on how it fits your leadership style and the needs of your team.

Whether the advice is immediately relevant or offers a new perspective, the real value comes from experimenting with each idea in daily practice.

By trying out these tips and observing their impact, you will find what truly enhances your performance as a leader and helps your team grow with confidence and clarity.

Top Tips for Inspiring Leaders

This is a fast toolkit for busy leaders. It contains short prompts. Clear actions. Use it to reset your day, prep a tough conversation, or plan a sprint with your team. It works well as a shared playbook.

Inside, you will find quick wins for meetings, feedback, and focus. You will find prompts that clear your head when the noise builds. You will find ideas that create momentum week by week. The language is simple, so your team will remember it.

This pocket-sized book is packed with daily tips, lessons and wisdom you can use for yourself and your team. Reflect on each suggestion, practise it and adapt it to your unique circumstances.

There is no one-size-fits-all solution for leadership, but you do not have time to make every mistake yourself. Learn from the experience of others and use their insights to shorten your learning curve and become a more effective leader.

Pick one idea each day, apply it to your next meeting or challenge, and watch your leadership and your team's performance improve.

How to Use These Books Together

The CEO's Compass, the most recent and comprehensive of these books, is your essential guide for navigating real business challenges. Start with it. Score yourself across the eight Quotients, honestly marking both your strengths and blind spots. Track your progress each month so you see real momentum, not just intentions.

Reach for *Inspiring Leadership* to fill out your approach. Bring your own standards to life in plain words and share them with your team. Invite your colleagues to write theirs so you build a culture of open expectations and shared commitment.

Add *Top Tips for Inspiring Women Leaders* to your toolkit. The ideas are flexible and can help you and your team break through daily barriers or fine-tune habits that truly shift culture.

Keep *Top Tips for Inspiring Leaders* in your pocket or within easy reach. Start making these tips part of your team's regular routine: each week, take twenty minutes to discuss one prompt together, agree on a behaviour to focus on, and keep a list of team norms visible to all.

Think of the two pocket books as powerful, shareable resources. Many leaders keep well-thumbed copies, highlighted and marked in the margins. If a team member is struggling, open a page together—there's almost always a tip or a piece of wisdom that suits the moment.

Stay connected

Leadership does not happen in isolation. Share these books, spark conversations, and reflect together on what is working in your world. If these tools help you, pass them on.

Join the newsletter for regular updates and new resources and listen to the podcast for weekly stories and lessons from leaders who have faced and overcome real tests.